ORGANIZING YOUR HOME AND LIFE WITH ADHD

Get Organized, Take Charge of Your Life, Improve Focus, and Succeed with ADHD in 15 Minutes a Day with Practical Exercises and Real Life Stories

Kai M. Jordan

swenett books

Copyright © 2024 Kai M. Jordan

The content contained within this book may not be reproduced, duplicated or transmitted without direct written permission from the author or the publisher.

Under no circumstances will any blame or legal responsibility be held against the publisher, or author, for any damages, reparation, or monetary loss due to the information contained within this book, either directly or indirectly.

Legal Notice:

This book is copyright protected. It is only for personal use. You cannot amend, distribute, sell, use, quote or paraphrase any part, or the content within this book, without the consent of the author or publisher.

Disclaimer Notice:

Please note the information contained within this document is for educational and entertainment purposes only. All effort has been executed to present accurate, up to date, reliable, complete information. No warranties of any kind are declared or implied.

Readers acknowledge that the author is not engaged in the rendering of legal, financial, medical or professional advice. The content within this book has been derived from various sources.

Please consult a licensed professional before attempting any techniques outlined in this book.

By reading this document, the reader agrees that under no circumstances is the author responsible for any losses, direct or indirect, that are incurred as a result of the use of the information contained within this document, including, but not limited to, errors, omissions, or inaccuracies.

For every individual navigating the dance between chaos and order, and for the resilient spirits seeking harmony in the midst of ADHD's unique challenges. This book is dedicated to you – may it be a guide, a source of inspiration, and a reminder that within every struggle lies the potential for a beautifully organized life.

With empathy and encouragement,

Kai

"In the midst of chaos, there is also opportunity"

SUN TZU

PREFACE

Welcome to the journey of transforming chaos into clarity, and finding serenity within the whirlwind of life with ADHD. As a woman who has weathered the storms of disorganization and distraction, I embark on this exploration with you, armed with personal experiences, professional insights, and a passion for creating a space where ADHD can thrive.

In these pages, we will venture beyond conventional advice, delving into the nuances of ADHD-friendly organization that transcends the boundaries of a tidy home. This is not just a guide; it's a companion on your quest for a life that aligns with your aspirations and reflects the unique beauty of your mind.

I invite you to embrace this journey with an open heart and a willingness to experiment. Together, let's navigate the intricacies of time, space, and the boundless potential that lies within the ADHD mind. May this book be a lantern illuminating the path to an organized and fulfilling life, tailored to the rhythm of your vibrant spirit.

As we embark on this exploration, remember that progress, not perfection, is the destination. Each step forward is a triumph, and each organized space is a testament to your resilience. Let's discover the joy of organization, celebrate the victories, and revel in the beauty of a life well-ordered.

With anticipation and camaraderie,

Kai

CONTENTS

Title Page
Copyright
Dedication
Epigraph
Preface
Introduction

Your Free Gift	1
Chapter 1: ADHD-Friendly Strategies to Get Organized	5
Real-Life Story # 1	22
Chapter 2: First Things First—Learn the Art of Prioritization	29
Real-Life Story #2	33
Real-Life Story # 3	40
Chapter 3: Now, Its Time for Organizing	46
Organizational Tips for the Home (By Area)	55
Chapter 4: Time After Time	69
Real-Life Story # 4	71
Real-Life Story # 5	79

Chapter 5: Digital Decluttering	88
Real-Life Story # 6	89
Chapter 6: Money Management Strategies	103
Real-Life Story # 7	106
Real-Life Story # 8	116
Chapter 7: Digital Distractions	121
Real-Life Story # 9	122
Conclusion	131
Thank You	133
References	134
About The Author	137
Books By This Author	139

INTRODUCTION

Of all the accolades and qualifications, I have been blessed enough to achieve in my life so far, there is one that towers above all others in its ability to open and close doors. It permeates through everything, and if you are reading this book, you most probably have this qualification too:

It is a Doctorate in Distraction, or *P.a.d.H.D*!

Do you know that feeling of having to redo your laundry for the third and fourth time because you forgot that you had put your clothes in the washing machine? By the time you remember to take them out days later, they have become mouldy, and you must turn the machine back on and rewash them! Or that feeling of having your immediate surroundings constantly collapsing into chaos the moment you merely exist in them: It's not even like you're trying to pick a fight with order but living with ADHD simply poses additional challenges for those trying to live an organized life.

Please don't take my word for it; you will witness real-life people living with ADHD sharing their experiences, which have escalated to the point of reaching out for professional help in getting Organized. Suppose anyone can understand the frustration that provoked you to pick up this book. In that case, it is the individuals you will meet on these pages: situations you can relate to. Solutions that you, too, can implement. Science that you can trust.

In the beginning, you had no idea how or where to begin. Your morale isn't being helped by thinking back to the last time you started, only to end up living amongst rubble again. I know the feeling of frustration that comes when others feel the sense of achievement: You have just spent the entire day cleaning up and organizing your living space successfully, but there's an accompanying feeling of futility because the only question on your mind is how long you will be able to maintain this fairy-tale of neatness this time.

That is where the recommended exercises in this book, which have helped others, will now set out to your rescue. Your intentions to become an organized individual are sincere; however, we must proceed with caution and vigilance due to the symptoms of ADHD that are waiting to ambush you as they ambushed our participants during the course, iterating solutions that work.

I collaborated with people whose ADHD symptoms range from mild to severe. I gained so much insight by hearing their stories and identifying the main culprit when it came to the ineffectiveness of conventional organizational strategies. We tried the standard strategy, and the ADHD always found ways to break them. By analyzing how and why the typical strategy failed, we were able to put the plan back together again in a way that is designed to be optimized for people with ADHD. This formed the basis of the 15-minute exercises presented at the end of each chapter: a hard-won victory, which we invite you to share by applying each exercise in your own life.

It will take some changing habits and learning new routines to help you keep your gains when it comes to being organized. If you can just use 15 minutes of the hours, you would have spent doom scrolling through TikTok and Instagram to implement the strategies you will learn here—your life will become all the richer for it.

It is also crucial to understand that ADHD minds work differently: A study conducted by the University of California-Irvine in 1996 found scientific proof that ADHD is a neurobiological disease that affects the D4 dopamine receptor in the brain (Armstrong, 1999). These are the parts of the brain associated with "novelty seeking." This means that nothing can turn off an ADHD brain faster than a tedious and repetitive task.

Not to fret! We will have you well prepared for that. If it's stimulation the mind seeks, then stimulation it will get as a built-in part of our robust strategy, and one added benefit of this is that you could end up *enjoying* the experience of maintaining the order you are about to unleash into your living space.

You will hear the experiences of those whose ADHD had driven them to their wit's end, eventually reaching out to me for specialized techniques to deal with ADHD once and for all. The solution manual is in your hands: the means to finally reign down the order, and you'll need to spend 15 minutes a day to keep it.

Decluttering, Organizing, and Tidying

Before we begin, it is essential to understand that different elements create and maintain an orderly space. As you start this journey, you will probably need to do all three. You only need to do two or even just one of these steps as time passes. If your living space's landscape resembles Armageddon's aftermath, we will take this as our point of departure and set out the guiding steps to cater to the most extreme possible cases.

Decluttering

Decluttering is needed when starting from ground zero. You're surrounded by what looks like the rubble from the apocalypse, and you need to get the space in order. You instinctively know that before thinking about getting anything in order, you must throw some things out or give them away. This process of deciding on what to keep, what to give away, and what to throw out is what is meant by "decluttering." To have a functional space, you first must ensure that what is in that space needs to be there.

Organizing

Once you have decluttered and know what you need to keep in each space, you need to decide where to keep it.

This is the step known as "organizing." A clear decision is made on where each item is supposed to go in a way that serves its function (you wouldn't put your daily toothbrush in the garage, for example). So, thinking about how you use things, how often you use them, and where and when you'll need to use them will help you most in organizing.

Tidying

The final stage is tidying. Tidying is simply putting things where they belong: It requires no decision or mental exertion of any kind, and this is the part where many people with ADHD may falter.

Decluttering is exciting and engaging and deciding what goes where in the organizing stage can also be exciting and empowering (you're essentially bossing your future self around). The tidying part is quite frankly dull to the ADHD brain but neglecting it for long enough is how we find ourselves in a situation where we must redo all three steps again because the mess we've amassed has become so colossal.

In the same way that people pay monthly rent to continue living in an apartment, tidying is the new rent we must pay to continue living in the orderly oasis we're about to create. That rent may seem expensive, but it is the price that everyone must pay to keep their spaces neat and clean; that much is obvious. But the nuance that hasn't previously been discussed concerning ADHD is the effects in which a moment of impulsivity at a separate location can have a direct impact on the deterioration of the organized structure you would have created at home.

Tips to guard yourself from these insidious habits will appear in the text, along with the explanation, when appropriate.

I'm sure that maintaining an organized space sounds like a lot of work. Some of you think, "But what's in it for me?" It turns out that there are a lot of perks you've been missing out on for long enough that I'll do the honours of reminding you:

- No more running an hour late because you couldn't find your car keys and had to call an Uber, which took another half an hour to pick you up.

- No more declining invitations to go out because you haven't done your laundry and have nothing good to wear.

- No more pretending to be homeless because you're too embarrassed for people to see the mess you live in.

- You'll probably find a reasonable amount of lost cash (so you'll technically get paid).

- No more needing to find something urgently and remembering seeing it but not being able to remember where, so you end up emptying drawers and cupboards and causing a complete mess, and then simply shoving that mess into the nearest out-of-sight location later when you don't feel like dealing with it.

- No more daunting feelings that prevent you from getting your space in order, so much so that you read every bullet point explaining why this is a good idea.

Something as simple as getting organized, ADHD executive dysfunction and all, can do *so much* in terms of improving your quality of life. Unfortunately, nothing cures hyperactivity faster than needing to do chores. Suddenly, you feel like you don't have any energy left. That's the same point we had to start from.

I hope that seeing the transformations and personal experiences of others who wanted what you wanted but could never reach it until now and their success stories can inspire you to follow along and do the same.

❖ ❖ ❖

What to Expect

Often, conventional techniques of organizing fail when applied by people with ADHD. Though some of the fundamental principles remain the same, the strategies outlined here are tailored for those with ADHD. You will learn methods that will help you get started on your journey to order and tips for maintaining that order once it is established.

We will break down some of the barriers that prevent you from staying organized and follow them up with remedies to overcome them, one exercise at a time. Each chapter will end with simple instructions for a 15-minute routine you can implement daily, so do not panic! Follow along and practice the exercises given, and you'll be an organized whiz quickly!

YOUR FREE GIFT

As a way of saying thanks for your purchase, I'm offering *The ADHD Relationship Evaluation and Money Management Worksheet* for FREE to my readers.

Plus, you will get *The Decluttering and Organizing Bundle* for FREE .

This valuable package includes four valuable components:

1. The Decluttering Booklet (42 decluttering exercises + 22 self-reflection pages + inspirational quotes).

2. The Decluttering Journal & Planner (30-steps to Declutter your home).

3. The Ultimate Decluttering Checklist

4. Let Go of Clutter: Supply Checklist, and Stay the Course Worksheet

To get instant access just go to:

http://swenettbooks.com

or Just Scan this Code by Your Phone

Inside the bundle, you will get:
- 42 practical decluttering exercises in the book in a printable coloured nice format.
- 22 self-reflection pages in the book in a printable coloured format.
- 262 pages of Decluttering Journal in a bright watercolour design.
- Perfect 30-step plan for Decluttering your home.
- Ultimate Checklist for Decluttering which will save you hours of your decluttering time and skyrocket your productivity
- Let Go of Clutter: supply checklist.

- Stay The Course Worksheet.

If you want to get the maximum benefit through your organizing your home journey, make sure to grab the free bundle **NOW**!

CHAPTER 1: ADHD-FRIENDLY STRATEGIES TO GET ORGANIZED

When the student is ready, the teacher will appear. –Lao Tzu

How It All Started

Steered By Stimulation

Before I begin by suggesting particular and completely counterintuitive methods that will mark the moment you finally start to understand why your struggle has continued for so long, let me first qualify how we got here: The story before the science behind the spontaneous adventure that became the much-anticipated ADHD Solution Manual for getting organized. This story starts with some hilarious anecdotes.

I was out for coffee with a group of friends, two of whom have ADHD. The topic of ADHD came up, and they began sharing some of the bizarre situations they had found themselves in, thanks to their diagnosis. First, my one friend shared that she had often sat in the car doing her makeup while driving.

My second friend interjected while laughing: Her story is hands-down the most extreme ADHD story I have ever heard. When she was younger, she discovered that she could watch videos on her mobile phone in her car while having the phone connected to the car's sound system using an audio cable. This would give her the fully immersive surroundings and proper movie theatre experience, all in the comfort of her car.

The problem is that she didn't restrict this theatre experience to when the car was parked. She had decided that it was reasonable for her to attempt to drive while watching Netflix in her car with her eyes darting between the street in front of her and her mobile phone screen.

There came a point where she had focused on the screen for just a second too long and had ended up veering off the road slightly, driving up the curb, and puncturing her front tire.

To anyone who asked her about how she punctured the tire, she told them something about her accidentally driving over a pothole, too embarrassed to confess the truth that she had veered off into the curb because she had been watching Netflix while driving. We laughed at her story until our eyes watered, but in all seriousness, that could have ended a lot worse!

The lesson we can observe from both stories is that when faced with a task that is incredibly routine and not engaging, the immediate response of the ADHD brain is to attempt to find ways of stimulating itself. If this is doomed to happen either way, it would make sense to volunteer that supplementary stimulation yourself, rather than end up in a situation where you're multitasking in a way that is unproductive or even dangerous.

From Reaching Out To Research

I started to notice an increasing volume of emails from people who have ADHD and are struggling to get organized, stay organized, or at least be able to live in a place that's presentable enough to have people visiting without them being traumatized by the ADHD go-to natural habitat of unsightly, functional havoc.

The call to action for virtually all these emails was a plea to help create organizational strategies tailored for people with ADHD. Recalling the fascinating anecdotes from my friends at the coffee meet-up, I began to respond with proposals. I am a professional in the field of life coaching and assisting people to get organized is what I live for.

I have authored literature on the topic of organization before. I haven't met halfway with those I intend to help, allowing them to step into my meticulously planned and organized life and, in return, ask them for permission to step into their world, experiences, challenges, and stories.

As we engage and gather an understanding of what the day-to-day struggles of living with ADHD are from the people who are the most qualified to talk about it, I invite you to witness a journey that perhaps is more important than the positive outcome it achieved.

This book has breathed new life into the questions many people with ADHD ask. In opening up, these individuals with ADHD have allowed me to try to understand their struggles to build innovative solutions together. If it were not for their aid in immersing me in their world, this book and its answers would not have been possible.

The crowning achievement of the 15-minute exercises that were developed and tested with direct input and feedback from those who have ADHD: The diligence that drove me to find those effective solutions was inspired by the stories and the intimate struggles that I was previously unaware of, that people diagnosed with ADHD endure daily.

Some are notably hilarious, others are sad and solemn, but they all share the "eureka moment" that closes each chapter. Some ADHD-diagnosed volunteers' stories and relevant life experiences have been included as italicized text. These participants who offered us their aid, extra help, and direction will appear as the pseudonymous alias "*Aid-E.H.D. #.*"

If you also have ADHD and have given up on all hopes of enjoying your very own organized, clean, and inviting safe space someday, that hope might not be so far-fetched. As you follow along, watch as we try the standard advice, debrief, and analyze why it fails for those who have ADHD, and then attempt our very own revised ADHD organizational strategies and tips.

This book will set out to finally confront your questions with the actionable answers you deserve. Without further ado, we'll start by addressing the issue of struggling to get started.

Setting Expectations

Before we continue, and to be honest and realistic about what you can expect when implementing these strategies, we must acknowledge that evidence is stacked against us.

Research findings claim that the inability to manage an organized life when diagnosed with ADHD is due to lower levels of persistence (Durand, 2020). Though it may prove true that sticking to one single strategy consistently and continually is a weakness, this should never deter you from utilizing these tips and techniques as much as you can whenever they come to mind.

Having a week or two where you fall back into old habits doesn't permanently disqualify you from ever daring to get organized again.

These occasional slip-ups provide you with an opportunity to prove to yourself that if ever you find yourself back in the messy environment of the old days (i.e., after you read this book), you are now empowered with all the knowledge and tools you need to tame the chaos when you notice that it needs taming.

A marked improvement is still an improvement, and you are encouraged to adopt those parts that stick out to you as your new habits and will have the most significant impact on your day-to-day life. This will make learning the habit come more naturally and have a more permanent effect.

Tools to Tame Your Chambers

Body Doubling

The first thing I want to remind you of as a form of encouragement is that you are not alone—quite literally! The first technique is known as "body doubling." Yes, it is highly effective for people with ADHD, and no, it isn't a secret ADHD superpower, although it does sound like it could be.

Body doubling is a way to invoke the power of accountability when trying to motivate yourself to do an aversive task that requires your attention, albeit to carry out some mundane routine. Being distracted from the task at hand is extremely easy when sitting alone. What makes it worse is that there are never any immediate consequences for procrastinating or simply not doing what you had set out to do.

The main idea behind "body doubling" is to initiate a

video call with your body double when you intend to start doing the task you're trying to avoid. As the video call begins, you and your body double share with each other what your goals are for the next hour, or 15 minutes, or whatever time you both agree to. You could, for example, tell your body double that you plan to fold the laundry, put another load of dirty clothes in the washing machine, iron two shirts, and polish your shoes.

It doesn't matter whether your body double is doing chores, coding some software project, or learning a language online. It isn't a competition. The point is to state what you plan to do and then use the live feed so you can keep an eye on each other. When the agreed time arrives, you both check in with each other and share how much of your goals you achieved as you had said you would.

You'll be much less likely to constantly check your social media while doing a task if you know that you will be held accountable if you are seen checking your social media and unable to complete your set tasks.

We also tend to underestimate how many times we surrender ourselves to distraction. You now gain mutual advantage as you and your body double help each other achieve what you set out to do using the subtle threat of punishment through social embarrassment if you don't do as you said.

There are websites such as Focusmate.com, whose primary purpose is to act as a tool for matching strangers worldwide with a body double. Are you dreading folding the laundry? Simply connect with your body double, and you will find inspiration to start on camera.

Your options at that point are just to begin the task or try to handle the most extended, awkward silence of your life. Video calling friends body doubles can also work if you have a supportive and encouraging circle of friends.

We have now addressed arguably the most challenging part: how to get started when you don't feel the motivation, inspiration, or energy. Think of a body double as a set of jumper cables that can give you a jumpstart when your battery is flat and have you running on all cylinders within minutes.

You don't *have to* want to do what you need to do to do it. Outsource your motivation: Your body double's job is to make you want to do it, and it works every time, particularly if they're a stranger. Now, all you need to do is show up.

Dealing With The "Doom Pile"

I'm not sure if adults with ADHD are either telepathic or whether they're secretly convening meetings to make sure they're all on the same page, but each of the individual volunteers we met up with during this project had a "doom pile" somewhere in the apartment or the house. For those who don't know, a doom pile is a pile of assorted items placed in a pile somewhere in a room, hoping that the pile will one day be sorted.

The pile can consist of books, clothes, art supplies, and equipment parts for some niche hobby.

The idea seems to be that if you're holding something and unsure where to put it, you can add it to the doom pile and figure out where it goes later. This speaks to the issue of "boredom intolerance," which is another term I learned during my internship with the ADHDers (people who have ADHD) and one that I respect. Intolerance of boredom is one characteristic that makes ADHDers some of the most exciting people.

To address the issue of the doom pile, we will cover a technique we've dubbed the "blitzclutter" in the following chapter. Doom piles bare evidence of the hyperactive trait of ADHD. In this instance, a drive to keep things moving, albeit not in a constructive sense. These piles are also a symptom of a space that has yet to be thoroughly organized.

As soon as every item had been assigned its designated place, we saw that the doom piles ceased appearing. Another secret to achieving this result was purchasing a durable, affordable basket for each room where doom piles appear. Now, instead of tossing the thingamabob onto an unsightly pile on the floor, you can pop it into the basket and use the blitzclutter technique to clear out the basket once per month.

Doomsday

We have spoken at length about doom piles but have yet to discuss the initial steps in dealing with them. We often find that there is roughly one doom pile per room. We recommend that you not try to deal with more than one doom pile per day, as it can be mentally exhausting. The first step in dealing with a doom pile is to split it.

There are usually apparent categories that each of the items falls under. One could be art supplies; another could be technology; toiletries are another; detergents and cleaning products are another category, and so on.

Once you have split the pile into smaller piles, you will be able to apply the blitzclutter method that will be presented in the following chapters. The technique isn't simply shown here because we must first explore and practice planning and creating workable plans. Our experience with volunteers showed that anything short of addressing the doom pile in a single effort was demotivating.

In other words, waking up to a single doom pile and then going to sleep with, say, five doom piles does feel like you've just created a more incredible mess for yourself, even though those piles have been categorized; hence, you are advised not to tackle the challenge until you have first been appropriately armed with the blitzclutter technique to come.

Aversive Task Management

Because the minds of ADHDers thrive on novelty, engagement, and stimulation, tasks that don't engage with these aspects of the mind are classified as "aversive tasks." These are the tasks that initiate the system shutdown for the ADHDer, and I have left dozens of voicemails trying to reach them and remind the ADHDer that they need to be attended to at some point. The best way to face the music is through the music. Music, podcasts, or audiobooks are a pleasant and stimulating experience. If we can strike a balance between things we want to do and the stuff that we don't want to do but must get done regardless, then we can address the problem of aversive tasks.

A constructive way of achieving this balance is to pair up the time you have assigned for decluttering, organizing, and cleaning with listening to either an audiobook or a new music playlist. The audiobook option is highly recommended since it can be set to play. At the same time, you get a lot of cleaning done without requiring input. In contrast, the music playlist can become a distraction itself. I have heard stories from one of our volunteers who fell into the trap of hyper-focusing on creating a playlist for almost two hours without getting any actual work done.

Suppose you plan to pair tedious tasks with stimulating ones from the outset. In that case, you will begin to look forward to doing them.

In general, the ADHD mind is wired to avoid aversive tasks such as chores and other similarly repetitive and mundane tasks. Pairing an aversive task with a reward helps offset the unpleasant feeling of the aversive task. Sometimes, it isn't possible to pair up the reward with an aversive task because it requires so much of your concentration, for example, when organizing.

In this case, it would be better to do the aversive task first but then immediately reward yourself with an enjoyable activity budgeted for in terms of time allocation. These delayed, conditional rewards can be like watching an episode of your favourite series.

So far, we have focused our discussion on the reward system of the brain, and this is fundamental: If we cannot find ways to ensure that decluttering, organizing, and tidying is fun from the very beginning, then chances are that you're unlikely even to attempt to implement the actual techniques to come.

Planning and Scheduling

The Self-Enforcing Nature of Schedules

Having given you a basic understanding of the issues related to time that you will likely face as an ADHDer, it is essential to know the difference between a daily schedule and a daily plan in the context that they will be used here. The schedule refers to the fixed routine essential for functioning; otherwise, your life would cease functioning correctly.

This includes attending class, working, eating, sleeping, etc. These things simply must be done consistently, regardless of whether you feel like it on that day, because the consequences of not doing them far outweigh the unpleasant experience of just doing them.

If you don't feel like going to work one morning, for example, and you aren't sick, then the consequences of showing up the following day and explaining that you hadn't come in the day before because you weren't in the mood could potentially be you getting fired.

Without a job, you would lose your income and ability to look after yourself financially (your bills, rent, monthly gym membership fees, online monthly subscription charges, and so on would keep coming in), rendering your life dysfunctional.

So, in considering this possible outcome, it is much less of a misery to go to work when you don't feel like it than to deal with the grief of having no income and trying to find a new job (because, again, it is less painful to have a job than not to have one). So, the consequences of your scheduled activity have a way of enforcing themselves through inflicting impartial consequences. If you don't eat because you're too lazy to get up and make food (we have all been there, that is fine. Nobody will force you to get and make food.).

The consequences of your laziness will be the severity of your hunger. The longer you postpone getting up to make food, the more intensely that hunger will harass you until, eventually, the pain from the hunger is greater than the pain of having to mobilize yourself to make some food to eat. The only alternative is ordering food online, which will incur a financial penalty as this food tends to be unsustainably expensive as a habit.

The Problem with Personal Plans

A plan includes all the activities and exercises detailed in this book. Plans are things like a daily to-do list that you need to find openings in your daily schedule to complete. Unlike disregarding the items in your schedule, the consequences of ignoring your planned objectives are not immediate and, therefore, aren't self-enforcing.

The problem with this is that ADHDers are prone to taking risks. Suppose the consequences of not doing an aversive task are delayed. In that case, those consequences are treated as though they don't exist.

You should know this from your personal experience if you have ADHD. All these routine chores that worry you for a few split seconds: "I should really pick up that clean stack of laundry that I folded yesterday off of that chair and pack it away in the cupboard," and then you immediately forget about it. In this case, the laundry has been washed. It has dried. It has even been folded and stacked neatly on the chair.

It would take less than 30 seconds to pick up the stack and place it in the dresser. The problem is often that there are no consequences to not putting your clothes away. Washing the clothes was necessary because dirty clothes are unhygienic. Drying them was also essential because you cannot wear wet clothes without getting sick.

Folding them was required because if you didn't, the clothes would be wrinkled when you eventually wore them, which would look unpresentable. However, this last step has no clear, immediate consequences other than being an eyesore. Tallying up the time of all the moments of thinking about packing that clean stack away would end up being longer than the task of just getting up and doing it.

The problem is that this incomplete task now takes up mental airtime, reminding you that it hasn't been done. This marks the beginning of a "mental doom pile": an assortment of incomplete tasks that you plan to complete, but since there are no immediate consequences to not meeting them immediately, they are added to the mental doom pile, taking up airtime as your brain juggles between thinking about one incomplete task to and another.

The effect of this is feeling demotivated. You'll spend just 30 seconds picking up the folded stack of laundry from the chair and putting it away; this will also mean that you must go through the other abandoned items and remain incomplete, all sitting in that mental pile.

Hence, the racing thoughts are exacerbated: a hundred

different thoughts of a hundred things you plan to revisit and complete.

Mind fleeing from one thing to another before retiring from that one also, all the while not taking any action to deplete the mental doom pile. An average person might look at the clean laundry stack and wonder how someone cannot complete such a simple and quick task. Where they perceive that solitary task, an ADHDer perceives it as a single part of the whole pile. The task is doable, but the pile is daunting.

Through sitting and speaking to our volunteers, I was fortunate enough to come to a place where I really and truly understood what drives them and what they find to be demotivating. My hope in sharing these insights is not only for relatability to ADHD readers but also to encourage involvement in applying the exercises through the example of my willingness to understand the challenges our volunteers and ADHDers, in general, face when attempting to follow conventional approaches.

Personal plans are items that you make time for within your daily schedule. An ever-growing mental doom pile haunts the consequence of not following through with those plans. Your thoughts will run from pillar to post continually and possibly even torment you when trying to go to sleep. Putting in the time to attend to these tasks is the only way to declutter that mental doom pile. Comprehending how these small, incomplete tasks affect the ADHD brain far more negatively than a neurotypical brain can be used as a source of motivation in ensuring that you never begin a small task without completing it. Treat it as a sort of allergy: An ADHD mind is allergic to incomplete tasks because those tasks have a propensity for forming mental doom piles that will clammer for your attention throughout the day.

To-Do Lists

Now that we know the dangers presented by mental doom piles, we can recognize the importance of having things written down. The difference between making a mental note of things you need to do on a particular day versus writing those things down in a list is that one will trigger your allergy, whereas the other will not. Taking mental notes is an activity we know will only create a mental doom pile. In writing things down, we declutter that mental doom pile and confine those thoughts to paper.

Every time you write something down, realize that you are decluttering your thoughts by offloading them onto the paper. Those things are the paper's problem now. The paper's job is to remember and keep track of them, thus relieving your mind from the burden.

A daily to-do list should comprise no less than two but no more than five items. This seems ridiculously short; you may even wonder whether something so brief could ever be practical. Our approach is that of a sprinter, not a long-distance athlete. By focusing on fewer, shorter tasks that are completed daily, we end up with the same results as though we had dedicated an entire weekend to doing spring cleaning.

The brevity of the itinerary also removes the daunting feeling you might experience if faced with a proposal for a five-hour decluttering, organizing, and tidying program. It also eases you into picking up new habits incrementally. You won't feel like you have instantly had this grand life transformation after exercising.

Still, when you look back to the person you are now in a month, you will notice how much you have changed. Consistency is the key. Make it a point to ensure that everything on your daily to-do list is done before going to bed. The items will be short enough to squeeze in just before bed, should you need to, but do not wait until the following morning because, you guessed it, a mental doom pile!

Depending on the speed with which you read this book, the exercise you read at the end of each chapter should automatically be added to your to-do list for the following day. Attempting to complete more than two of the end-of-chapter exercises on the same day is not recommended. This is because the aim is to change behaviour and habits, and it is more effective for you to focus on the lessons from each exercise and reflect on the experience of implementing them.

To-Do List Pitfalls

As much as to-do lists are a very easy-to-implement solution, we must remember that there is much truth to the saying, "Old habits die hard!" Your allergy can creep up on you anytime, as our volunteers showed us. But we have solved the issue, so you don't need to learn from your experience.

REAL-LIFE STORY # 1

"I was so excited to be added to this project! Not only was I going to finally get all this nonsense cleaned up, for once and for all, but this time, I was going to get personal coaching to help me keep it tidy. Yeah, I'm not going to lie—I was blushing when the team walked in and had a look at my indoor mountain ranges stuff. Still, this is precisely what Kai, and the team were looking for. If I'm not the worst-case scenario, I'm sure I'm close to it, lol! Anyway, I had to explain the doom piles, and Kai was taking notes! Bless her heart. This turned out to be a lot better than what I thought I had signed up for. I thought they would just help me clean, maybe leave a pamphlet on organizing, and then leave. I was happy to take that offer. A clean place within a week is not a bad deal, considering its state! But Kai and the team genuinely really wanted to help me specifically. They tried to learn more about the ADHD side of things, took notes, and asked me some questions I hadn't thought about before. It was flattering, to be honest.

So, the first issue was the dreaded 'to-do list.' I was given some homework on the first day to write down three things the following day before they arrived in the evening again. I never thought I would get stuck on step one. So, I wrote down to take my boyfriend's dog for a walk, sign up for this body-double website Kai told me about, and do some physical exercise. My boyfriend stays just down the road with his two dogs, just by the way.

So, I did two of the three things, but when it came to exercising, that was a bit of an issue. I thought putting down was a good idea since I've always wanted to start healthy habits, but I sort of got distracted. So, I had to Google 'exercises for beginners.' Then I started learning about how you need to work a different part of your body each day and how you need to have a weekly gym routine to cycle between the different body types. I spent a whole hour doing research without doing any physical exercises. Still, Kai understood it and showed much interest in working together to see where things went wrong. We ended up figuring out the issue, and I'm grateful that Kai and the team are concerned enough to want to help find out exactly what the drawbacks are for me, ADHD and all." –Aid E.H.D. #1

After debriefing with our first volunteer about what happened with the to-do list exercise, we found that the old tendencies of mental doom piling crept up in this exercise. By writing something too broad for a to-do list, you essentially postpone defining the specifics of that item to when you need to do it.

When it came time for the physical exercise, our volunteer was confronted with a doom pile of exercises on the internet. She then had to spend valuable time sorting through it all before she could even think of starting with the exercises.

ADHDers have the incredible capacity to go incredibly deep into topics. Their seemingly endless curiosity means that anything too general or vague added to a to-do list could trigger a hyperfocus episode (another known symptom of ADHD) to define the specifics. Instead of writing down broad items like "do physical exercise," writing something more specific, like "do 100 sit-ups," is a better plan.

The to-do list items need to be so clear that you could stop what you're doing right now and do one of the items without thinking. The specificity makes the list simple for ADHDers, making it much more manageable. Examples of things that can be written on a to-do list are

- Wash the outside of the car with soap and water.
- Vacuum the inside of the car.
- Wax and polish the outside of the car.

Notice how each of those actions is extremely specific. Suppose someone had written "wash the car" as an item on the list. In that case, that item is open to interpretation as it could mean just washing the outside with soap and water, or it could also mean doing all three items from the list above.

This could mean the difference between a task that takes 15 minutes and one that will take over an hour to complete. The secret advantage here lies in long-term consistency. Washing, vacuuming, and polishing the car requires such a considerable dedication of time and effort that it's simply easier to avoid doing it entirely. However, splitting it up into washing the car on the first day, vacuuming the inside on the following day, and polishing it on the last day, you would have achieved the same desired result, and each of those steps is reasonable enough for you not to be overwhelmed by it.

A final tip involving to-do lists is to try to have various

items depending on your energy levels. For example, putting down washing the car and vacuuming the vehicle as items on a to-do list for the same day isn't recommended as those are both high-energy tasks.

Pairing a high-energy item with a low-energy item works well because you can complete the tasks consecutively if you have the energy on high-energy days. Still, when your energy levels are low, you could start with the lower-energy item and then attend to the higher-energy task later in the day when your energy levels pick up. You could be in high spirits when you write the list. Still, it is always important to consider the variability of your mood. You need to be able to split up the items if you need to and have them still all be doable on your worst days.

Focus Zones: Your 15-Minute-Long End-Of-Chapter Exercises

As mentioned at the very outset of this book, the goal is to provide practical, actionable advice, particularly for ADHDers. The bespoke lessons learned from our volunteers allow you to benefit from the combination of my organizational expertise and their lived experience as people who deeply understand what it is like to try and navigate organizational methods with ADHD.

To get the most out of this book, it is highly recommended that you stop at the end of each chapter and wait until you have had an opportunity to complete the Focus Zone exercise before continuing to the next chapter. The aim is to change habits, which can only be achieved if you work through the 15-minute end-of-chapter exercises prepared.

ADHD-Friendly Strategies: Focus Zone 1

The Goal of This Focus Zone

- Implement the body-doubling technique.
- Create a week's worth of simple To-do lists.

Focus Zone 1 Procedure

1. Set a timer for 15 minutes.

2. Write a list of 21 small tasks you must complete that week (don't include anything that would already form a part of your daily routine). You can take up to 5 minutes on this task.

3. Split your list of 21 tasks into three sections by writing the number 1, 2, or 3 next to each item. It would help to balance it out so that you have seven items of each number. One indicates easy tasks, two indicates intermediate items, and three shows relatively tricky tasks.

4. Group the items in three sets, ensuring each group has a task marked 1, 2, and 3.

5. You should now have seven groups of three. Mark the first group with tomorrow's date, the second with the day after tomorrow, and so on, until you have assigned dates for each group of three spanning over the next week. (You should be roughly 10 minutes into the timer now.)

6. For the final five minutes, either sign up for any free body-doubling website or app of your choice or message a friend you think would be willing to body-double with you as you coordinate your schedules to go through your to-do lists. (It is advisable to use a body doubling app, such as Groove or the platform Focus mate, as this will make it easier to set up other activities with people who are available at concise notice, and this might not be possible to do consistently if you're relying on one specific person.)

7. For the next seven days, use the to-do list to

familiarize yourself with how to use the body-doubling app you selected to complete all the daily tasks marked on your daily to-do list.

Key Chapter Takeaways

- Use body-doubling when you're struggling to get started with a task.
- Pair aversive tasks with pleasurable activities.
- Split your daily to-do list into three tasks per day: easy, intermediate, and complex.
- Do not be broad in specifying to-do list activities.
- Write tasks down to avoid creating mental doom piles.

The following chapter focuses on prioritizing and the first stage of transformational organization: decluttering tailored to suit ADHDers.

CHAPTER 2: FIRST THINGS FIRST— LEARN THE ART OF PRIORITIZATION

Fools learn from experience. I prefer to learn from the experience of others. –Otto von Bismarck

Having succeeded in numerous failures when it came to maintaining a clean and orderly living space for any extended period, the person I assisted in this second case eventually decided to sit down and analyze why their default settings seemed to produce pandemonium. Fortunately for you, the role of the person going out and learning by experience "the hard way" has already been played: gathering lessons from the unpleasant experience so that you can savour the same smug grin that must have lit up Mr. Bismarck's face when he first uttered that quote. Psychiatric medication goes a long way in remedying many of the symptoms that make living life with ADHD so colourful and eventful. What the medicines won't solve automatically is the propensity toward impulsive behaviour and the agitating urge to keep things moving at a breakneck pace.

Having ADHD is like running a bustling airport with airborne planes that all need to land. Because they can't possibly all safely land simultaneously, we often focus on the aircraft with the most significant emergency. If you have ADHD, you probably don't see any problem with that logic. The real problem is that not everything urgent is necessarily essential. This is where we need to learn the art of prioritizing. There are four categories of things that need to be attended to:

- Some are urgent and important.
- Some are urgent and unimportant.
- Some are important but not urgent.
- Some are not urgent and unimportant.

They are prioritizing means to list things in order of their importance appropriately. An example of something urgent and vital is submitting your work or school assignment in time to meet the deadline. Something critical but unimportant is when your work colleague has left things to the last minute and now requires your help to meet *their* deadline. This may be important and urgent for them, but it isn't as essential for you to. This inability to correctly identify when things are critical and unimportant is what often leaves people with ADHD overwhelmed, as we end up leaving essential tasks unattended as we preoccupy ourselves with the adrenaline of assuming that urgent tasks mean high priority.

Side Quest: Priority Cheat Sheet Exercise

When you next find yourself in a situation where you're feeling overwhelmed and aren't sure how to proceed or what task you need to focus on first, grab a scrap piece of paper and a pen and follow the instructions below:

> 1. Draw two intersecting lines across the center to divide the paper into four quadrants.
>
> 2. Using the bullet points above, write out each bullet point as separate headings in each of the four quadrants.
>
> 3. Begin to fill in each of the tasks you think you need to do based on where they should fall in the quadrants.
>
> 4. Your workload now is reduced to only the items in the "Urgent and Important" quadrant.
>
> 5. Everything else is temporarily not your problem. Focus on completing the tasks under the "Urgent and Important" heading.

This might seem irresponsible at first, but the reality of our condition is that with this inability to prioritize things that need our attention appropriately, we end up finding ourselves petrified by the burden of the unrealistic requirements set before us, knowing full well that completing that buffet of demanding requirements is unreasonable for the average person. So, we avoid getting started on anything altogether, procrastinating for just long enough to hopefully activate our ADHD superpowers that grant us the capacity to work at double or triple the average speed. We summon every efficiency tool, executing well-rehearsed shortcuts.

At the same time, another YouTube video plays in the background, guiding us through another method that we could use to speed things up even more. It is like having a secret love for the thrill of jumping off the highest of cliffs and then scrambling to start building an airplane on the way down.

Astonishingly enough, these dare-devil incredible feats of mustering up the last-minute ultimate motivation to deliver on outrageously absurd deadlines vindicate individuals who have ADHD sometimes. The problem then becomes that success itself. These episodes convince us we can do the unthinkable when pressured.

In hours, we completed what others had been working on for days. Suppose we had spent as much time getting started on the work instead of spending time hyper-focused on mastering obscure shortcuts.

In that case, we might be able to experience a deadline where we submitted without being out of breath. To illustrate how viciously these tendencies can brutally ambush you at precisely the time when you cannot afford to be a victim, below is a true and unfortunate anecdote from one of our volunteers.

It vividly demonstrates how catastrophic things can become when disorganization is casually dismissed as something you think you can learn to live with.

REAL-LIFE STORY #2

"In my third year of study at college, I had left an assignment for the last minute, and I pleaded with the lecturer via email that I may be granted permission to submit my assignment on the day of the exam, which was the following day. I breathed a sigh of relief and even told my neighbour I could get this concession. I arrived in good spirits, well-rested, and well-prepared for the exam the following morning. The second my eye caught sight of my lecturer, I remembered that I had forgotten my laptop with my assignment back in my room. I panicked and requested an Uber to collect my laptop from the room. Uber was still running and waiting for me outside when returning to my room. I realized I didn't have my security gate key for the room. I saw it through the window, and it dawned on me that in my haste, I had forgotten the keys inside when I left that morning.

Quick, fast, and in a hurry, I began tugging at the dead branches of a nearby tree. If I could find a branch long enough, I could stick it through my room's open window, fish my keys out, get my laptop, and head back to the exam venue. While I stood at the window, branch in hand, trying to fish out my keys, my neighbour arrived and asked if I wasn't supposed to be writing an exam. At that moment, I suddenly understood what is meant by 'the calamity that life gradually becomes when living with untreated ADHD.' Even after retrieving my laptop, the annoyed demeanour of the Uber driver was punishment in and of itself. The crescendo of anxiety was knowing that I was about to get riddled with glares from the other students for walking into an exam late. My late arrival would translate to less time to write the exam.

I never thought I could ever get so publicly attacked by my mental health issues. I was ambushed from all sides that morning. The symptoms of my ADHD, which I had learned not to take too seriously, had ambushed me in the most public spectacle. I didn't feel embarrassed and incompetent; that whole fiasco proved my incompetence to everyone! From my lecturer to the Uber driver to my neighbour to my classmates, all these people got the worst impression of me that day. How can anyone be so disorganized? How was I arriving late for an exam I had studied for? Why on Earth was I making the driver wait while I was gathering branches and doing suspicious things to gain access to a dorm room?

That situation wouldn't have happened if I had not waited until the last minute to do the assignment. Had my room been tidy, I wouldn't have missed my keys sitting on a pile of assortments when I left. That fiasco would never have happened if I had planned and packed my laptop the night before. A monumental failure of a situation occurred because I was getting too comfortable and did not sense the urgency in making a more significant effort to be organized and maintain an organized space around myself. Please do not wait until it's your turn to be ambushed. Learn from my experience. This was the catalyst that led me to seek the intervention of an organizational expert." –Aid E.H.D. #1

For every struggle, we forged a solution. For every tragic anecdote, we prepared a contingency antidote. The two main obstacles holding back this case were a fear of letting items go (decluttering) and establishing an ongoing new habit designed to improve impulse control.

Decision Dilemmas

Thinking of a big task like organizing your living space can feel overwhelming. Where do you even begin? The first problem you run into is the apparent lack of urgency. You have survived so long in a mess that the urgency to get things sorted has lost its influence. What harm could another year of functional chaos do? You know that it is essential, but when you look at the full scope of the task, it is easy to lose motivation to start.

This presents the irony: To be diagnosed with a condition characterized by hyperactivity, and yet when we need to use that energy, it abandons us. In any other situation, we can zoom and dash about as though we're the unofficial mascots for the rat race.

Still, when it's time to get ourselves organized, our allergies kick in as our brains compute a roster of rational excuses. This is when you can utilize your ADHD mechanics to your advantage: If something isn't urgent, you can *make it compulsory*.

Urgency is just a time limit that is fast approaching. Instead of thinking of how you will clean an entire room, you can simply focus on a single drawer at a time.

Side Quest Exercise

1. Set an alarm for five minutes and focus on cleaning that single drawer or cupboard for those five minutes.

2. If there is anything in that drawer or cupboard you haven't used in the past six months and are unlikely to use in the next six months, you can throw it out or give it away.

3. Focusing on one drawer or cupboard daily for five minutes gives you a sense of urgency since you are racing against the clock. It also means that in a month, you will have covered 30 different drawers and cupboards that are now entirely decluttered!

4. Using the test question of whether you have used or will need to use something in six months is also a great way to quickly reach a verdict on what you can throw out without overthinking things and getting trapped in analysis paralysis.

5. The time limit is also effective in curbing your distractibility. Five minutes is not enough time to start looking through the photo album you just found or reading through your old journal.

6. You can simply focus on completing the task at hand first, knowing there will be ample time to look through what you'd like to see once the five minutes is up.

The first ADHD hurdle we encountered with this standard technique is that there are too many items to decide how many to throw away. It seemed like a lot of work since there mainly were junk/nonessential items in many of the drawers, so we simply inverted our goal. Instead of looking at an entire heap of things and trying to decide what to throw away, you can flip the whole process on its head through prioritizing.

The "Blitzclutter" Decluttering Technique

1. Begin by setting down a newspaper so as not to dirty the floor.

2. Simply empty the drawer or cupboard you are decluttering completely onto the newspaper.

3. First, select the items you *need to keep* functioning.

4. Take each of these items and place them back in the drawer.

5. On your second scan of the items, select the items you think you would only buy once in the next six months if you were to throw them out.

6. Likewise, take each of these and place them back in the drawer.

7. The items that remain in the newspaper are now classified as garbage.

8. Scrunch your newspaper with the junk inside and dispose of it in the bin.

Remember that the more items you hoard, the harder the task of organizing will become simply due to the sheer volume of items that need organizing. You'd like to make the subsequent steps as easy as possible, and a big part of that involves cutting down things that are taking up space that don't need to be there.

Everything that remains in the newspaper can be scrunched up and thrown out. When you've accumulated a lot of "stuff" approaching your decluttering, or blitz cluttering, this is a lot more effective (and faster!) than having to go item by item trying to decide what you have the heart to throw out.

A fundamental principle to remember is that reduction leads to organizational efficiency. If you only have five containers in the cupboard, as opposed to a dozen, not only will it be much easier to keep your cupboard clean, but your fridge will be a lot tidier as well.

Since you only have five containers to store leftovers in, you'll be more inclined to eat those leftovers to free up your containers instead of adding to the stockpile of leftovers in the fridge. So, by letting go of things, the result is that you are less wasteful and make better use of the things you still have. Less items also means it will be a lot easier not to lose things.

I would not recommend blitzcluttering to a neurotypical person. Still, with ADHD individuals, the risk of possibly throwing out something that might be needed gets offset by a capacity to improvise and think creatively and quickly. In other words, you will take that potential outcome in your stride.

A completed decluttering job for a room makes you feel excited and anxious, like a child who has found a lost kitten. Will that decluttered space be maintained, though? Not quickly if you have ADHD. Again, we have discovered the shortcomings of standard strategies and observed how Aid-E.H.D. #1 broke it to enable us to share the ADHD-compatible revised version.

Counteracting Complications: Pause the Impulse to Purchase

The space we had blitz cluttered about six months prior had relapsed back to the rubble we saw when we entered that room for the very first time. Impulsivity is another well-known symptom of ADHD. It is insidiously subtle, and unless you are actively trying to recognize its contribution to the recurring mess, you're likely to miss it. Below is an informative recollection from our volunteer who retraced their habits and identified a stumbling block that adds another spanner to maintaining a clean and orderly environment once the order has been established!

REAL-LIFE STORY # 3

"We had completely decluttered my room, and I felt quite proud of the transformation. As time passed, I was seduced into hoarding my mobile phone. On three occasions, I was out of the house without a charging cable. So, I would buy one from the nearest electronics store without a second thought. Fast forward six months, and as I looked across the landscape of my assortment-littered room, I noticed that the first things that would have to go in my second decluttering attempt were the four charging cables that served no purpose, all in the same place. I only needed one." –Aid E.H.D. #1

Resisting the impulsive urge to buy something in the frenzy of a rush is an integral part of maintaining a tidy environment. These extras get lost among all the other extras you already have among the extras of even more things! We collectively refer to such redundant extras as a mess: the very same mess that we're trying to banish for good.

In the context of living with ADHD, you should think of decluttering as a two-part process: the first part is sifting through your belongings and getting rid of the items that you don't need, and the second part involves making it a habit to take a moment to pause and think carefully whenever we make any purchase that you are likely to take home.

Suppose you already have the item you are considering purchasing at home. In that case, you are effectively buying garbage since you must throw it out when you need to declutter again. Conversely, the fewer redundant items you impulsively buy, the less frequently you will need to declutter.

Managing Stimulation Hunger

A great strategy that will help you to prioritize the task at hand while staying focused is what I like to call "getting in character." Part of what turns off our brains when it comes to mundane tasks is their lack of novelty. As we have seen so far, it doesn't take much to intentionally trigger some of these stimulating reward systems in an ADHD brain. "Getting into character" might sound silly at first.

Still, its benefits are twofold: it will keep you excited and stimulated by the novelty of cleaning while constantly reminding you not to get distracted.

Getting into character is as simple as putting on a pair of rubber gloves when cleaning or wearing an apron so as not to dirty your clothes. Wearing boots and eye protection goggles when cleaning the garage or spraying cleaning chemicals is another excellent example of getting in character.

To demonstrate why this method is highly effective, let's use a hypothetical example: You have put on your rubber gloves for your daily five-minute drawer cleaning exercise. Suddenly, your phone rings, and you have a notification. You are far less likely to stop what you are doing and take off your gloves and your eye protection goggles just to check what that notification was for. It is less of a hassle to complete your focused five minutes of drawer cleaning first and then check your phone notifications afterward.

Whenever anything attempts to steal your attention, the rubber gloves will continuously act as a visual reminder that your main priority is the five-minute cleaning task. Everything else can wait.

This also alerts those around you not to interrupt, as they can see that you are fully committed to the task. They wouldn't want to hassle you and interrupt your workflow to show you a funny video or engage with you for anything that isn't so urgent that it cannot wait for those five minutes.

Remembering to Remember

If you don't currently own rubber gloves or a cleaning apron (it is highly recommended to invest in a pair of rubber gloves), another trick you can use is to wear bangles or a watch. When you begin your five-minute cleaning exercise, take your jewelry, or watch and put it on the opposite wrist.

This will be a constant reminder to focus on the five-minute cleaning task, as the awkward, slight discomfort will constantly prod you to check whether you are still doing what you need to do. Swapping your jewelry or watch to the opposite wrist each time you put the laundry in the washing machine is also an excellent habit.

With ADHD, it is often a case of "out of sight, out of mind." We must rewash the same laundry five times and forget it sits in the machine for days. Suppose you switch your jewelry or watch to the opposite wrist as you fill the washing machine.

In that case, you will be constantly reminded of the entire day to go and check the laundry. Putting a ponytail or bangle on your wrist can serve the same purpose for those who don't wear any jewelry. The idea is to trigger the novelty of wearing something a little off that will prod your brain as a reminder to take out the clean laundry, so you don't have to try and remember to yourself actively.

First Things First: Focus Zone 2

The Goal of This Focus Zone

- Declutter a single room in a week by using the blitzcluttering technique.
- Use the urgency importance matrix to decide when the next best opportunity to declutter is.

Focus Zone 2 Procedure

1. Draw an urgency importance matrix as illustrated in this chapter each day when you arrive home or at the beginning of the day if you work from home.

2. One of the items in one of the quadrants includes the blitz clutter technique on a particular drawer or cupboard of a room you would like to work through decluttering that week.

3. As you cross off tasks in the urgency importance matrix, continue to reassess when the blitz cluttering technique reaches the highest priority of the remaining tasks.

4. Once blitzcluttering reaches the top of the list, set a timer for 15 minutes.

5. Implement the blitzcluttering technique using the instructions outlined in this chapter for the duration of the 15 minutes.

6. Repeat this exercise daily for a different drawer or cupboard in the same room until all compartments have been wholly decluttered.

Key Chapter Takeaways

- Use the blitzcluttering technique to declutter a space, one compartment at a time.
- Use "getting into character" to help you manage stimulation hunger and stay focused on the task.
- Swap your jewelry to the opposite wrist or put jewelry on the wrist to remind you of tasks with a waiting period (like the washing machine).
- Controlling impulsive buying helps to reduce future clutter.
- Use a priority matrix to help you decide which task to attend next.

In the following chapter, we will look at how to diagnose what type of organizing style best describes you and how to organize specific rooms in your living space.

CHAPTER 3: NOW, ITS TIME FOR ORGANIZING

Oh! Old rubbish! Old letters, clothes, and objects that one does not want to throw away. How well nature has understood that she must change her leaves, flowers, fruit, and vegetables every year and make manure out of the mementos of her year! –Jules Renard

If you were to ask a well-organized person in their apartment where you could get a pair of scissors, they would respond with something like, "If you go upstairs, you'll see the second tower of drawers from your left, and if you open the third drawer from the top, you'll find a pair of scissors in the purple pencil case," and they'd be right! If you asked a disorganized person this same question, their response would be, "Well, the last time I saw them, they…" There are two things wrong here. First, you should be able to find a pair of scissors in the place where the scissors go. Second, "The last time I saw them…" implies that the person saw the scissors at some point at an arbitrary location that wasn't designated for storing them.

Not only that, but the person saw the scissors there and didn't immediately pick them up and return them to where they were supposed to go.

In the first scenario, it would have taken less than two minutes with an organized person, and you would have had scissors in hand. In the second scenario, you get a response of where the scissors were last spotted. However, you still need to look for them yourself, potentially asking others if they have seen them or know where they are—it's almost like opening an investigation! For some context, in the first case, the scissors are found, presents get wrapped, and you're off to the birthday party.

In the second case, you're panicking and running late—the presents aren't wrapped because we're trying to hunt down those scissors.

You're sending a text to apologize for being late to the party. Imagine the difference in stress levels between those two scenarios. The irony is that it probably took longer to find the missing scissors than it would have taken to pack and organize the room itself.

When you visit a library or a record store with the name of an author or artist whose works you'd like to find, you know to go to the relevant genre section and then scan the selection alphabetically.

You can then tell whether the store has any of their work available. This is the magic of order: it gives rise to efficiency. It enables people to enter a place for the first time and navigate around it like they were raised there. Someone had to take the time to design the structure of that order, ensuring that it was functional and intuitive enough to maintain it far less than the work required to function in that space if it had no such order.

To set things in order is truly an investment that you need only make once, and you will reap the benefits for as long as that order is maintained.

Step One: Housewarming Party

Now that I have your attention and adrenaline pumping—You panicked, didn't you? One of the symptoms we observed with people who find it challenging to keep a tidy place is anxiety about having people coming over. No, I am not about to propose that you host a housewarming party.

A common trait I noticed with most of our volunteers is that they prefer to keep themselves isolated in their living space (at least, that was the case until we transformed the place).

This is understandable if the place is embarrassingly messy. Still, the problem with hiding the issue and never allowing anyone in is that this only worsens matters because you grow accustomed to living in chaos and not seeing anything wrong with it.

Social interactions can serve multiple purposes, including accountability. Although our volunteers were slightly embarrassed when we entered their residences for the first time, they were all quite excited when we came for the follow-up assessment. The maintenance wasn't perfect, but it was more than tidy and orderly enough to have people over for a visit.

Even if it means having just one or two of your closest friends or family whom you invite in for tea or coffee from time to time, as opposed to fleeing the scene of the crime against orderliness to have a coffee with that friend at a cafe, this allowing of people into your living space is just enough motivation to help you want to maintain your new standards. Even in cases of people who don't necessarily struggle with organizing and keeping a place tidy, you may often find them doing a bit of extra cleaning and tidying up when they are expecting visitors.

Form Follows Function

In the previous chapter, we spoke about decluttering and focused on ensuring that all remaining objects and belongings in your living or workspace needed to be there. Now that all the items that posed a high risk of recreating the chaos have been removed, we need to organize those that remain.

The best way to do this is to remember the axiom: "Form follows function." This means that where things are placed and how you decide to pack them depends on what makes functional sense for you since you are the one who will be using the space.

This is also where you might need to perform an exercise that we dubbed "time skip." We found it helpful, mainly if you haven't organized an area from scratch. We found that often, our volunteers didn't know how to decide on how best to allocate spaces for items since things were generally placed "nearby." Sometimes, an item had three or four potential locations where it was "likely" to be.

Purpose Hygiene

One of the most striking similarities we found in the volunteers who battled to get themselves to maintain the newly organized space was disregarding what we came to call "purpose hygiene." Organization is based on the idea that everything has its proper place. Similarly, every activity done within a space has its appropriate place and sticking to these helps to make your task more accessible in terms of staying organized.

For example, you are far more likely to clean your dishes and place them on the dish rack afterward if you prepare your food and eat it in the kitchen. However, preparing a meal and bringing the cutlery, bowls, glasses, mugs, and plates to your room where you can eat while watching a series on a laptop has already initiated a problem.

You're unlikely to return the utensils to the kitchen immediately after eating, which now means you have a habit of relocating items to areas you were never told to have them in.

It seemed inconsequential at first, but we soon realized that unless we made it a point to learn to be continually mindful and intentional about using areas specifically as intended, the habit of absentmindedly not returning things to their spot would continue to pose a problem.

The most rewarding part about organizing your own space is that you can structure it in a way that best suits your preferences. There is nothing wrong with wanting to enjoy a series on your laptop while eating food. All this would need is to reorganize the kitchen area so that you can place your computer at a safe distance so as not to get food onto it, but close enough that you can watch your show as you eat. This way, washing the dishes afterward becomes a lot more convenient.

This simple mealtime activity shows that organizing

effectively can help you still do what you'd like to while dictating how those tasks are done to make doing what you *need* afterward easier.

Time-Skipping Exercise

"Time skipping" is an exercise we developed to have a solid basis for determining the most efficient structure for organizing items in any given space. The procedure is as follows:

> 1. Select a room to be arranged.
>
> 2. Write down several things you would do when entering that specific room. For example, for the bathroom, you could write down: shower, brush teeth, use the toilet, dry hair, do makeup.
>
> 3. For each activity written down, do a quick walk-in rehearsal of the action to trace your steps. Take specific note of where you stand when doing the activity and at which point you would need to retrieve items to do the activity. For example, when doing makeup, you would need to stand in front of the mirror and have your makeup bag with you. Brushing teeth would have you standing by the sink with your toothbrush, floss, mouthwash, etc.
>
> 4. Locate the nearest storage place for the item you use at the position you use it. In our case, it was revealed that it made no sense to keep the makeup bag in the bedroom when it was only used in front of the mirror in the bathroom. Storing it in the cabinet under the sink was a

better way of organizing. This way, it doesn't require carrying it back and forth and risking leaving it somewhere.

Another advantage of the time-skipping exercise is that it revealed all the items being stored in areas where they were never used.

Anything stored in the bathroom cabinet for the sake of storing was, in fact, clutter. If it serves no function and isn't used often, it only gets in the way of trying to reach for the essential items. Growing accustomed to seeing things occupying spaces where they serve no purpose is what lays the groundwork for normalizing chaos.

The "Launch Pad"

People with ADHD often misplace things. That sometimes causes the mess in the first place: desperately rummaging through things to try and locate lost car keys, cell phones, and other urgently needed items. Not only does this contribute to the return of chaos, but even if the mess caused by the frantic searching eventually gets put out of sight, it is rarely put away in an organized fashion. This means the closest empty place is where the items end up. It's a quick solution, but precisely the sort of thing that will cause you to rummage through the unsorted bundle of random objects again since anything could have been accidentally placed anywhere.

The "launch pad" station is the first part of the solution. Instead of placing your keys, wallet, and cell phone in the nearest spot, you hope you'll remember allocating a small tray near the front door will establish a new routine that will solve the misplacing of those essentials.

When you enter the house, you know to place your phone, wallet, and keys on the launch pad. The same applies when you're ready to launch out of the house. Those three items tend to be the ones you cannot leave the house without, and they're the usual culprits for provoking people to search frantically until they're found.

ORGANIZATIONAL TIPS FOR THE HOME (BY AREA)

Bathroom

We'll begin with these area-focused organizational tips by starting with the bathroom. The bathroom offers one of the best showcases of inherent corporate style.

It can help you to diagnose which style is best suited for you and which would be most effective to implement throughout the rest of the living spaces.

- **The visual organizer:** If you are a graphic organizer, you will find that frequently used items are often left out in the open on countertops instead of stored out of sight. This doesn't necessarily mean that the space must remain untidy. Remember that the goal is not to punish yourself for enforcing unnatural behaviours but to alter your inherent behaviours to be conducive to an organized environment. For visual organizers, this means designating places for items within line of sight but presenting them in an organized fashion. This means using clear jars neatly placed on shelves for separate items like earbuds, bath bombs, and floss. Affordable small shelves with suction cups can also be attached to the shower wall to hold shampoos, conditioners, and body wash. The idea here is to still have the items within your line of sight for easy access but to have them placed intentionally in a tidy manner that frees up countertop space for you to do routine surface cleaning and maintenance.

- **The hidden organizer:** If your bathroom countertops are primarily clear and frequently used items are mostly stashed away in drawers and cupboards, you fall under the confidential organizer classification. An immediate advantage of this style is that everything appears neat and organized on the surface; however, having things out of sight doesn't necessarily mean they are organized behind closed drawers! The best remedy is to divide your drawer and cupboard spaces using smaller transparent containers. I like to refer to the larger of these containers as a "get-ready bin." This would include items like makeup, daily medications, items for your daily facial regimen, and anything else that you would make use of every day in your routine, all packed in a convenient smaller container that you can take out, use, place everything back into and then store away out of sight. The contents of the container itself needn't be meticulously organized, and the items have already been categorized. Categorizing is a valid form of organization. The only thing you'd need to keep in mind when using this organizational technique of categorizing is that the contents of the container or compartment you have allocated need to be few enough that you don't need to empty the entire contents and cause a mess to find an item you are looking for. Secondly, suppose you do have to open the container to find an item. In that case, the contents need to be few enough that placing all the items back in immediately isn't a hassle. Here, we are talking about taking less than 30 seconds to remember all the items back in the container if they are emptied. The goal here is not to add another tidying-up task to your routine but to simply have a quick-fire way of storing things away in an organized fashion without you having to overthink things.

- **The detailed organizer:** This is the absolute extreme organizer type, and although this may not be you, there are still some lessons we can learn from this organization style that you might want to incorporate in your household. A detailed organizer uses subdividers and labels in every cupboard and every drawer. Everything is the antithesis of a doom pile. There is a container for dental items, another for bath-related items, and another for shaving cream, razors, tweezers, and other items. Each container is not only categorized, but each serves a particular purpose.

- Suppose a specific task needs to be done, like brushing your teeth. In that case, the dental container immediately comes out. It guides you through the process, as the toothbrush, toothpaste, floss, and mouthwash are all there. A clear benefit of this system is that it makes it extremely easy and convenient to pick up healthy habits. By compartmentalizing tasks, you can automate entire processes since all the thinking and planning are done beforehand. Taking out a container is tantamount to issuing the order to execute all tasks involving the items in that container automatically. Whereas before, you might only brush your teeth before bed, you now have the healthy routine of flossing and using mouthwash added to that process. The same can be said of the container that houses your facial scrub, toner, and other skincare products.

Kitchen

The part of the kitchen with the most clutter for some people is the fridge. We noticed that some people have powerful ethical feelings surrounding throwing away food, and this means that they end up with stacks of containers with leftovers, most of which have gone wrong, crowding their fridges.

A more practical solution for those who cannot throw food away is intentionally giving it out while it is fresh.

Our volunteer bought a bulk package of containers to store in the pantry next to the kitchen. When she notices that she has cooked too much or has leftover food, she puts it into one of the containers and puts it in the fridge. The following day, she reheats the container and gives it to someone needy on her way to work.

Not only is she now routinely doing a good deed, but it is the innovative solution that meets all her needs. It exemplifies that being organized helps you do exactly what you want to do, but more efficiently. Her fridge was clean and clear, a hungry person was fed, and she exclaimed how she felt so much better leaving the house and knowing that she was starting her day with an act of kindness.

Lounge/TV Room

An essential function of being organized is always to remember that the purpose of this valuable tool is always to make everything more efficient, as opposed to existing merely as a punishment. This means that, despite what has been said thus far concerning purpose hygiene, it is vital to remember that the system established exists to serve the user: form follows function.

We are all aware that often, there is a family tradition and culture around eating meals together in the TV room. Although one can argue that food, strictly speaking, is not to be served in the TV room, the essential element of family bonding that occurs around these times means that we can make certain exceptions in this case.

This does, however, mean that a solid structure and rules governing how these special mealtimes are enjoyed must be firmly established. An example of such a rule that works most effectively is that as soon as the credits appear, everyone who has finished eating either clears their dishes to the kitchen or the delegated person assigned to clear the dishes brings them to the kitchen.

If anyone is still eating, the same rule applies for the second program, and by the end of the second program's credits, all dishes must be cleared from the room. If any dessert is to be served, the same would apply to the eating of that course. This simple rule helps to avoid a situation where dishes pile up in the TV room, and by the time dishes need to be done, there is an overwhelming heap of dishes to be cleared and washed.

The temptation is to leave them piled in the sink until morning because it is simply too late to start washing all the dishes. For small families, having the children learn to rinse their own plates and cutlery before placing them in the dishwasher or sink is recommended. This teaches them responsibility and relieves the workload of whoever has been assigned to wash the dishes that day. Still, turning on the dishwasher at the end of the evening is far more manageable.

Observing and trying to keep the storage space in the lounge/TV room to a minimum is essential. This is a counterintuitive fact, but the function of this room is to either watch TV or entertain guests. There is a minimal number of items that serve a real purpose toward that end other than remote controls, gaming consoles, and gaming controllers.

This means that this room's storage spaces should be filled primarily by these items alone. Having too much excess storage space in the living room is a primary culprit in becoming a hidden location for the clutter of the worst kind: children's toys, stray coins, random keys, various business cards, pamphlets, and so on.

The fact that these storage spaces are the only ones available in this room makes it that much harder to fight the temptation to quickly grab the nearest eyesore and shove it out of sight when visitors are about to come over. This generates the worst kind of clutter as these are generally valuable items that cannot be thrown out, but that will be very taxing in terms of them eventually being moved to their designated places. So, suppose you have the luxury of having enough space to reorganize your furniture to have as few drawers and cupboards in the TV room as possible. In that case, it will result in a far less clutter-prone space in the future.

Garage

The exact antithesis of the lounge organization approach can be seen when it comes to the garage. It is most advisable to set up extra storage space in this space. This can come in the form of mounting additional shelves along the walls, mounting overhead shelving from the ceiling if the overhead clearance allows it, and mounting a pegboard.

A pegboard is a large chipboard with holes predrilled an inch apart to let you hang power tools, spanners, screwdrivers, and other frequently used tools within reach. The garage also offers a great storage space for seasonal items such as Halloween and Christmas decorations. Airtight, clear, labelled containers are highly recommended as this will allow you to store and retrieve the relevant containers without having to take down and open each container to find the requisite items.

Another obvious advantage to decluttering the garage is getting paid to get rid of unwanted items through a garage sale. In situations where you might feel like it is wasteful to throw valuable items out, a garage sale can put your mind at ease, knowing that the items will still be put to good use. This will also help you be more discerning regarding which items you decide to keep.

One final piece of organizational advice concerning the garage: For those who don't have a shed, designate a garage segment specifically for gardening tools and house maintenance items. This includes transparent, airtight containers for storing spare light bulbs for routine replacement. Placing these items in the same space as the screwdrivers you're likely to need when replacing burnt-out bulbs is the sort of forward-thinking that will make it easier to return them to their designated place after use.

Bedroom

As previously discussed in the purpose hygiene segment, the bedroom is not a place to eat and snack as it is too susceptible to become a site of stockpiled dirty dishes, which can lead to pests in the space. Ideally, the use of technology such as laptops should be kept to an absolute minimum as this can exacerbate symptoms such as insomnia, which ADHDers already must contend with in most cases.

Though you might save a laundry basket somewhere else, keeping a second one in the bedroom is advised. There are times when you might decide to change straight into pyjamas after a long day, and this is precisely when the doom piles begin to spawn.

Organizing a space to cater to your behaviour when you are at your worst is the best way to ensure that the order will always remain functional. By making allowances for instances when you may not be as motivated to stick to the rules, you help ensure that those more lenient rules are enforced. In other words, it is better to set lenient standards that you will abide by than to set stringent rules that you will likely fall into the habit of ignoring.

Organizing: Focus Zone 3

The Goal of This Focus Zone
- Create a functional schematic of the living space.
- Reorganize each living space room (Note: This

part of the exercise will only be practical if the blitz cluttering exercise from the previous chapter has been completed for each room!).

Focus Zone 3 Procedure

1. Set a timer for 15 minutes.

2. In those 15 minutes, take a clean sheet of paper for each room in your living space. On each sheet, sketch a rough schematic of the room. (It only needs to be accurate enough for you to understand where everything is relative to each other. In other words, all you need is the name of the room, an outline of its general shape, and an indication of where the door is in the sketch.)

3. Use the time-skipping exercise illustrated in this chapter to take note of the items you use in which positions the most when you enter that room. You can write the item's name at the position in the sketch where you usually use it. It would help if you didn't overthink this, as the first impression that comes to your mind will always be the correct answer.

4. Try to have a sketch for all the rooms completed within 15 minutes for this part of the exercise.

5. For the remainder of the week, set the stopwatch for 15 minutes, choose one room per day, and use the functional sketch you created to designate the best places to store specific items in the room. Once a storage location for an

item has been determined based on your sketch, you can group other similarly categorized items at the exact location as the first item for convenience.

6. Continue doing this exercise daily until each room in your living space has been reorganized. Remember to use your body-doubling tools as often as needed: they help!

◆ ◆ ◆

Key Chapter Takeaways

- Observing "purpose hygiene" is one of the first steps to getting into orderly habits.
- Remember that "form follows function" when organizing.
- Order is there to help you function more efficiently, not to punish you.
- Set up a "launch pad" to avoid losing keys and misplacing your phone whenever you enter or leave your place.
- Use the "time-skipping" exercise to help you identify how best to organize a room.
- Use the bathroom to identify whether you are a hidden organizer, a detailed organizer, or a visual organizer, and organize the rest of your living space according to your organizational style.

The following chapter will discuss a topic many ADHDers prefer to put off until later: time! We will explore the concept of "time blindness" and what measures you can take to make sure that you minimize the detrimental effect it has on you.

CHAPTER 4: TIME AFTER TIME

Don't be fooled by the calendar. There are only as many days in the year as you use. One person gets only a week's value out of a year, while another gets a full year's value out of a week. –Charles Richards

One of the primary symptoms of ADHD is executive dysfunction. A consequence is that we are notoriously poor at estimating the time it will take to complete tasks. This results in situations where we might miss flights because we arrived at the airport late after underestimating how long it would take us to pack, and we left it all for the night before the flight.

Since we are so used to moving at a break-neck pace and doing things faster than most people, we sometimes forget that some things take time, no matter how fast you think you'll be able to do them.

Part of that poor time estimation comes from our procrastinating. When doing things at the last minute, we get a much-needed boost of adrenaline that motivates us to take action.

Although this is sometimes enough to pull us through,

when this dangerously drastic method fails, it does so to the accompaniment of tears. Leaving things to the last minute will die you precisely when you simply cannot afford it to happen. One of our volunteers confessed to this relevant story that shows us the extreme measures you could feel compelled to resort to when wrong time estimation catches you lacking:

REAL-LIFE STORY # 4

"You must hear this one! The Christmas and New Year's Eve of 2021 was by far the most self-critical, or rather—let's just say one of those moments that shows you what you're like. You have this moment dissociating and stepping out of yourself so you can stand there and acknowledge that you are solely responsible for his disaster.

It was Christmas Eve, and a few friends and family members had gathered for the usual holiday traditions (cooking, baking, decorating gingerbread houses, etc.). I happened to be in the middle of typing some code I had been working on for a few days. I isolated myself and continued with my work until I was given an ultimatum: If I didn't come and contribute to helping with the preparations, I would be assigned to wash all the dishes alone *afterward. Without pausing to consider the projected heap of dirty dishes that so many people would create and without feeling how long it might take one person to wash dishes, pots, pans, and so on for a dozen-plus people, I agreed to wash the dishes if it meant I could continue with my work in peace. Dishes are easy. It should be quick. I'm also a fast worker, so three hours into washing dishes later that evening, I regretted it.*

It was an eerily familiar situation of finding yourself assigned an outrageously unreasonable volume of work, panicking and stressing, but never asking for help. (Volunteering was also how I ended up with the volume of work in the first place). Hands down, it was the wildest thing

I've ever done on Christmas: There were so many dishes that I devised a desperate last-minute plan. When I was alone by the sink, I started seizing the opportunity to quickly hide as many dirty dishes as possible and cutlery in the drawers, behind detergents in the cupboards, and so on. The idea was never to hide all the dishes but to stash away just enough to reduce my workload. I cheated, but I still found a way to get it done. Maybe it's the fear of knowing that menial chores always take a lot longer than you think that makes me avoid them altogether." –Aid E.H.D. #2

Time Budgeting Exercise

It would help if you began to sharpen your time estimation skills. How long does it take you to brush your teeth? How long do you shower and get dressed in the morning? How long does it take you to prepare and eat breakfast? These are things I had never even thought about until doing this exercise.

The time it takes me to get ready depends on the time and time I need to leave the house. When I'm running late, I simply do it faster; that is the sort of thinking that will leave you in a state of being disempowered as someone with ADHD. We already know that time estimation is our weakness, so let's work on that.

It may seem like a very inconsequential exercise, but you will probably be surprised by how long it takes you to get ready in the morning. Knowing how much can be achieved in 15 minutes a day becomes pointless when grappling to grasp precisely how much we can get done in 15 minutes.

Coming to grips with your ability to estimate time does a lot in helping you budget time and run different tasks simultaneously to be more efficient. For example, let's imagine you gained the knowledge from this exercise: You know it takes you an hour and fifteen minutes to get ready in the morning.

You also understand that your washing machine takes an hour to complete a wash cycle. Suppose you begin your morning by putting your dirty laundry in the washing machine just before your morning routine by the time you finish eating breakfast. In that case, the laundry will have completed its cycle in time for you to move the clothes from the washer to the dryer. Planning and coordinating these efficient parallel tasks are only possible when you accurately understand how long it takes you to complete them.

Take 15 minutes to break down your morning routine, your evening routine, and your laundry routine on a piece of paper. Break each exercise down into its constituent steps as demonstrated below, i.e., gathering laundry together, setting the washing machine, waiting for the cycle to end, taking clothes out and hanging them out to dry/putting them in the dryer, taking the dry clothes and ironing/folding them, and packing the folded clothes away.

Leave a space on the right-hand side for each of those steps to fill in how long it took you as you go through those steps with a stopwatch. This will immediately give you a powerful insight into which tasks take you the longest and which tasks you could perhaps cut down on in terms of time accepted to complete. It will also alert you to the functions with the highest distraction risk.

I have done this exercise myself, and I must admit that I couldn't get all the times down for all the tasks on my first attempt. Sometimes, I would forget that the timer was running when doing specific tasks or simply get distracted on my phone while trying to reset the timer. It took me three days of attempts to populate the stopwatch times correctly.

However, once it was done, I felt I had reached a new level of self-awareness after realizing how often tasks take me longer to complete because of getting distracted and scrolling through messages or emails while brushing my teeth. Remember that we have already accounted for a stimulation budget. This means that if the plan was not to brush our teeth while checking emails, we simply stick to the task, i.e., brushing our teeth. Anything less could result in delays and distractions, making other tasks take longer.

Pre-Exercise 1

> 1. Take your morning routine and break it down into steps, such as brushing your teeth, taking a shower, getting dressed, making breakfast, and so on. Every step that happens from the moment you wake up until the moment you need to leave the house or start doing work.
>
> 2. Write each step of the routine on a separate line with some space left on the right side of each line to fill in times later.
>
> 3. The following day, follow the checklist, and as you begin each activity, start your stopwatch.
>
> 4. As soon as you complete each step of the checklist, stop the stopwatch, and write down the time it took you to complete that step.
>
> 5. Once you have recorded the time, reset the stopwatch, and begin the next step until you have filled out the time required to complete all the steps.

Now that we have established two key elements of our strategy in the future, namely, stimulation budgeting, by pairing aversive tasks with rewarding activities, and the foundation for scheduling, using the newly discovered process that enables us to estimate the time required to complete tasks accurately, we can now begin to release the clarity and serenity of order into our living spaces. We must keep a realistic perspective on our progress as we do so.

The enterprise you are about to undertake is a large one and one that will not be completed all in a single day. Success will come through consistent application of the principles laid out here.

Installing a Clock Network

Time blindness, or time myopia, is another assassin bent on harassing ADHDers. Therefore, the timing exercise recommended above is something an ADHDer can improve on. This can bolster and benefit other organizational skills as well. Symptoms of time blindness include

- procrastination.
- I am getting easily distracted when attempting to switch between one task and another.
- An inability to judge the expected duration of a task reasonably accurately.
- Either you are being extraordinarily early or late for appointments.
- Difficulty in honouring set deadlines.
- Significantly shorter "time horizon" (a time horizon is how far in the future a person can plan).

These symptoms cause people to misinterpret these characteristics as simply "poor time management and disorganization."

It is highly convenient and helpful to always be aware of the time without pulling out your phone, which is a prime suspect in getting distracted before noticing it. A quick retrieval of your phone from your pocket to check the time should only take a few seconds. And yet there you are 10 minutes later, swiping left and right on dating apps or downloading a video meme so you can open it in your phone's editor because you just had a brilliant idea of how to remix the meme to make it even funnier.

I was genuinely impressed when one of our volunteers showed me the archive of memes she had remixed. It boggles my mind how someone could have that much energy and drive for such an eccentric and specific hobby. I digress, but I can understand how ADHD affects focus.

When people put so much energy into a fascinating spectrum of peculiar hobbies, it is hard to fight the urge to mention them in passing, derailing the focus. Even saying cell phones was enough to derail the initial point: Mobile devices are best left out of sight for as much as possible.

This is where having a network of clocks, one for each room in the house, will prove extremely useful. Being able to lift your head and immediately read a clock within your vision helps improve your time perception. It makes you immediately aware when you have spent too much time hyper focusing on something to the point of now running late.

The clocks will alert you when your schedule is slightly

off, allowing you to retrace your steps and discover what may have caused the delay. (For example, if you usually start cooking at 5 p.m. but notice that you're creating an hour later, figuring out where you lost track of time will help you identify the "high-risk" activities, i.e., the ones most likely to steal away your time without *notice.*

REAL-LIFE STORY # 5

"By far, the least fun time I ever have is when it comes time to take a flight. So, for some reason, to be completely honest, for ADHD reasons, I always seem to have something come up, such as missing my flight and having to pay penalties at the airport to book the following flight. On one of the rare occasions that I could be at the airport on time when leaving my apartment and returning for a work trip, I arrived back at the apartment only to realize that I might have misplaced my apartment keys at some point during my trip! Panic began to set in, and my mind was racing, trying to remember where I could have forgotten them. I couldn't recall any point during my trip where I would have needed to take those keys out for anything. All the keys on that keychain were related to things in my apartment. The only place they could have possibly been in my actual luggage.

Locked out of my apartment and with no other leads to go on, I began to open my luggage bags right there in the corridor outside my apartment to try and find these elusive keys. They were nowhere to be found! Exhausted and frustrated, I remembered a saying, 'If you can't find something where it is supposed to be, start looking where it is not supposed to be.' I had just returned from a two-week-long- trip. I knew that I had reached the airport on time when I left. I was in a rush, but I was on time, nonetheless. The unlikely but possible location of my keys suddenly came to mind. I tried opening the door of my apartment, and it opened! There on the inside of the door were my keys. I had been in such a frantic rush to get to the airport when I left for my trip that I had left my keys on the inside of the door, and my apartment, with all its valuable contents, was effectively completely unlocked for the entire two weeks, but luckily, I was the first person to discover it!" –Aid E.H.D. #2

The Sands of Time

Having a digital stopwatch on your cell phone, tablet, or computer effectively imposes a sense of urgency on a task. Still, the problem is that it doesn't provide a constant visual cue as to how well you are doing without having to take a momentary distracting break to check how much time remains. Even if you leave the stopwatch screen open and active, those running numbers still require some arithmetic calculations to interpret how much time has passed and how much actually remains.

The best solution is to have something physical and visual that counts a fixed amount of time that you can gauge briefly and know how much time has passed and how you are completing the task within the allocated time.

The Hourglass

Most people are familiar with the concept of an hourglass. I'm sure many of you have seen them used as fancy desk ornaments in offices or study rooms next to bookshelves and a small globe. For people with ADHD, having a physical hourglass has an efficient and effective use: to be able to visually see time passing briefly and to be reassured that the task at hand will eventually come to a definite end, thus motivating you to put your all into focusing your energies on completing said task before the sand runs out. It offers a great way to gamify your focus while racing against the clock. Thus, you are far more conscious of the temptation of distraction that you are generally prone to.

A Lesson in "30 Seconds"

Anyone who has played the game "30 Seconds" is familiar with the excitement that an hourglass can bring. It is precisely the factor of the 30-second time restraint that makes the game so fun. To those unfamiliar, 30 Seconds is a game where players are split up into two teams, and each team takes turns having one of their members pick up a card with five different things listed on it.

That person must describe those things to the rest of the team while their team guesses what they're describing. The catch is that a small hourglass is set to 30 seconds, and only the correctly identified things on that list within those 30 seconds are counted toward the team's score. The team with the highest score at the end wins.

This game teaches some critical skills, particularly to people with ADHD. Firstly, is the strategy: Because there is a 30-second time limit and each team needs to gather as many points as possible, going through as much of the list as quickly as possible is essential.

The team member describing the items on the list may find it difficult to explain specific points or, in some cases, may not even know what some items are and can not describe them. If there were no time limit, the team could end up stuck on the same item for hours, trying to find some lateral thinking solution to help them break down and convey what is written as best they can.

However, due to the time restriction, when the other team members can sense that the team player is struggling to find the words to portray what is on the card, they will quickly urge the member issuing the descriptions to skip the difficult one and move on to the next one. If the next one is equally challenging, they are encouraged to skip to the next one. The idea is to ensure that all the items on that card are at least attempted.

It is often found that time can run out trying to describe a problematic item. In contrast, there were far easier ones toward the end of the list that could have earned the team more straightforward points.

Suppose the team member issuing the descriptions is a good player. In that case, they will often scan through the card first and start with the items they believe they will have the easiest time describing to their team before moving on to the others instead of simply starting at the top of the list and running down the items sequentially.

Only when all the items have been attempted, and the 30-second hourglass is still running, does the member backtrack to take another attempt at the items that were previously skipped over. It may be a simple game, but it contains critical insights into approaching any task list that needs to be done within a given time frame.

The Hourglass Method

1. Scan through the list of tasks and assess which ones you can complete quickly and with

the least effort.

2. Please start with the most straightforward tasks and mark them as complete as you go along.

3. Review the list again and assess which tasks will be the most challenging and time-consuming. Leave these tasks to the very end.

4. Please go through the intermediate tasks and mark them as complete as you go along.

5. If you start with a task that you had initially assumed was intermediate only to discover that it is taking much longer than you initially expected, mark the task as incomplete and skip over it to begin a different medium task.

6. Once the intermediate tasks are either complete or marked as incomplete, reassess the remaining tasks on the list, including those you had initially marked as complex.

7. Reorder the remaining items on the list in order of the ones you believe you can complete quickly, considering the progress already made on the intermediate tasks.

8. Go down the rearranged list of tasks, marking each of them as completed once they have been completed.

9. Complete as many tasks as possible before the timer runs out. You win if you can complete all of them before the hourglass runs out!

Just as is the case when playing the game 30 Seconds,

whatever isn't done on the list by the time the hourglass runs out isn't done. You must move on.

This allows you to escape the trap of hyper focusing on a difficult task that could take such a disproportionate amount of time that it leaves you with no time to do other essential tasks. Remember that in the game of 30 Seconds, it doesn't matter how many items on a given card the team leaves incomplete. What is more important is how many items *from all the cards a team manages to complete* to win based on the total points accumulated.

Similarly, being able to complete 20 tasks in a day of playing a few rounds of "900 Seconds" (the constructive 15-minute ADHD version of 30 Seconds) is far more beneficial and productive than spending all that time hyper focused on a specific task that takes up a disproportionate amount of time.

As an ADHDer, your superpower tends to be speed. Keeping your momentum going makes you a force to be reckoned with. During our work with some of our volunteers, we found that when one of our volunteers was tasked with helping us reorganize her art supplies, she, unfortunately, ended up being sucked into hyperfocusing on tasks like sorting out her watercolour paints in the correct colour chromatic order.

Although this would have looked very pretty, it took up a disproportionate amount of time that could have been better spent sorting out the paint brushes and canvases. Gifting her a 15-minute hourglass the following day made a world of difference! Despite sometimes not being able to complete *all* the tasks listed for that 15-minute round of the game, overall, a lot more progress was made. Her fast-thinking mind, coupled with the visual cues provided by the hourglass, allowed her to perceive the current task in greater perspective and regroup her energies and focus when she sensed that she was perhaps putting too much effort into doing something that wasn't explicitly required from the list.

One final suggestion for using the hourglass method is that there will sometimes be tasks that are left incomplete by the time the hourglass runs out. This, too, is an added benefit! The reason is that you then can reassess the overall importance of that task.

Does it have to get done? Is there a way of simplifying it or stripping it down to its essentials to make it more doable? For example, designating a specific place for the watercolour paints was essential; however, colour-coding them was not. Therefore, that task could be reworded to be more precise (and far less time-consuming, too!), and the newer simplified task can then be added to a card for a new list. This way, you are constantly setting new achievable goals and reassessing the necessity of those goals while deconstructing them to the fundamental, functional core of what those goals each intend to achieve. You are constantly pruning the fluff from your to-do list, making the desired outcome more efficient and easily attainable.

Time After Time: Focus Zone 4

The Goal of This Focus Zone

- Create an accurate time budget.

- Install a clock network.

Focus Zone 4 Procedure

1. Set a timer for 15 minutes.

2. For the first 10 minutes, write down the tasks in your daily morning and evening routines, as illustrated in this chapter's "time budget" pre-exercise. Remember to leave a space to fill in the actual time to complete the activities later.

3. For the remaining 5 minutes of this exercise, take a quick walk around your living space and observe the many areas throughout the different rooms that do not have a visible clock within eyesight. Make notes of where clocks can be added as well as what sort of clocks would be most suitable and would work within your budget.

4. Use the remainder of the week to fill in the stopwatch times for the time budgeting exercise based on the tasks you specified in step 2, and to purchase the clocks required to install your clock network.

Key Chapter Takeaways

- To compensate for time blindness, a symptom of ADHD, creating a time budget is necessary.
- Installing a clock network is crucial in

maintaining a direct line of sight to a time display to counteract time blindness.

- Using the hourglass method will help be more effective in completing tasks and knowing when to move on.

This chapter primarily focused on time, and the place where most of us spend a lot of our time these days is cyberspace. As much as there is clutter in the physical world, there can be even more clutter in the digital space. Fortunately, the next chapter is filled with more ADHD-friendly, practical techniques for dealing with digital clutter.

CHAPTER 5: DIGITAL DECLUTTERING

Please get rid of clutter; it may be blocking the door you've been looking for. –Katrina Mayer

REAL-LIFE STORY # 6

"One of the absolute worst pieces of advice I have ever been given, and a piece of advice I followed for years, was one of these 'quick fix' digital decluttering 'hacks' that I got from a friend of mine in college. Mind you, it's worth mentioning here that this friend did not have ADHD, so in her defence, maybe this method might work well for neurotypical people, but for me, it was the beginning of an utterly unmanageable disaster that I technically have yet to fix to this very day.

How this all started was my friend had a look at my desktop, and to call it disorganized was an understatement. I had random folders containing files from old assignments, some music recordings from when another friend and I did a music jam session, and some random images I wanted to upload to my Pinterest. You get the picture. Just stuff everywhere.

I was overflowing on my desktop to the point where I had to change the sorting order just to ensure that some of the files I wanted would even appear on the screen. On seeing all this chaos, my friend suggested the 'sorting hat method,' apparently a Happy Potter reference that went straight over my head; excuse the pun. But the fact that she said I could have my entire desktop sorted within 10 seconds piqued my interest.

It went something like this: copy everything on your desktop except for the recycle bin, cut all those files and folders, create a new folder called 'To Be Sorted' on your desktop, and simply paste all the items into that folder. It was an absolute saviour of a solution—at first. The part I missed was where you had to put aside time to sort through the contents of that folder.

After using this method to declutter my desktop for the first time, I stopped naming the folder 'To Be Sorted.' I opted to call it 'Desktop 1' instead. You can probably see where I'm going with this—I eventually ended up with a 'Desktop 5' folder containing a 'Desktop 4' down to the original 'To Be Sorted' folder.

I had created a digital doom pile, within another digital doom pile, within another, and going five levels down. This was causing serious performance issues with my laptop, to the point where I simply decided to copy that 600-gigabyte doom pile to an external hard drive and simply search by file name if I ever needed a file." -Aid E.H.D. #4

The danger of disorganization when it comes to our digital habits is that the severity of bad habits is potentially infinite. In physical reality, the chaos we can potentially create is restricted by the physical space and the limit of the number of physical items in that space. In the digital world, new copies of items can be created in two clicks: one to copy and the other to paste.

Unused space can be constructed from thin air by creating a new folder. So, it shouldn't be that surprising that in the extreme case cited above, our volunteer was able to create a multidimensional digital doom pile that would have taken them so long to sort through that they found it easier to simply opt to banish the entire multidimensional abomination to an external hard drive.

Paperless Digitization

Digitizing important physical documents sounds laborious and complicated, but it is much easier than you think. It will allow you to throw away heaps of papers cluttering your spaces and that you're unlikely to ever get around to sorting until some crisis arises. Counterintuitively, sorting through these documents is a lot easier when they are digitized.

It is a lot easier to find exactly what you're looking for when you can simply use a keyword search function instead of having to rummage through mounds of paperwork and create chaos for yourself.

Remember that if you ever need a physical copy of your digitized documents, that is as easy as simply printing the document from your saved digital version. You can say goodbye to the anxiety of throwing away important papers.

To digitize a document, you only need to set it flat in a well-lit area and simply take a photo of it. And that's it! It's as simple as that. To organize the digitized document, it is recommended to use a cloud storage provider as this will act as a fail-safe should anything happen to the device the document was initially saved.

Creating separate folders for utility bills, insurance documents, investment documents, bank statements, phone bills, and so on is advised. Each file can be named starting with the date, followed by the description of the file. This naming convention also makes it easier to keep track of paid bills with payment receipts, as the digitized payment receipt can be named starting with the same date as the associated bill with the word "receipt" added to the end.

You can now start building up a database of all your important documents and have them each conveniently paired with their payment receipts when you sort them in alphabetical order. This also makes keeping track of unpaid bills much easier, as you can immediately see which bills have not yet been paired with a payment receipt by sorting them in alphabetical order.

Once a document has been digitized and the digital version has been synchronized with your cloud storage, you can discard the physical document, as you now have a backup. Whatever physical documents you require in the future can always be printed from a digital copy. Some helpful apps automatically convert captured photos into PDF documents.

It would be beneficial to download one of these because if you have a physical document that spans several pages, it is far more convenient to capture those several pages as photos and have them automatically combined and saved as a single PDF document than to have to rename and keep track of several separate photographs that are part of the same document. The PDF also makes it easier to print the full multipage document later, should you need to.

Decluttering Apps and Programs

The best way to free up a significant amount of space on your devices is to go to the list of installed apps and programs and sort them in order of their size. This will immediately show you which apps and programs are taking up the most space, and you can then weigh this against how frequently you use each of the apps.

If an item appears third in the list in terms of taking up the most space and you have only used that app two of three times in the past six months, you can probably live without it. Some of these scarcely used programs take up such a considerable amount of space. You will probably also find some programs and apps on the list that you may have installed but never used.

Uninstalling such software will not only free up space and help your device run faster, but you will have the peace of mind that, should you ever require that software later, you can always re-download it.

Be sure to back up any personal files you may have created in the software to a separate folder named the name of the software as a sub-folder to a parent folder named "Deleted App Backups," as deleting the software will usually delete all associated files created in the program as well. If you're ever unlikely to use those files again, delete them without a backup.

Once the bulk of the apps responsible for taking up the most space has been assessed and cleared out, as necessary, drawing your attention to other apps that aren't frequently used but still take up space on your device is needed. This can be done by playing around with the various sorting options available. Try sorting by ascending and descending date installed, last date accessed, alphabetical order, etc. This mixes up the list and allows spotting apps that may have flown under the radar when sorting by file size.

Linking Software Functions

If you were to link the word "repeat" with the word "create," you would get the new word "recreate," which combines the two words by chaining them together along with their meanings to create a new word that combines both. It's almost like a form of linguistic decluttering. Similarly, you may have an app on your device for video editing and a separate app for photo editing. Still, finding a single app that can perform both functions is possible. One app can serve the function of two or three.

This isn't always possible as sometimes collaborating with colleagues may require you to use software, but for personal use, you'll find that even if you only migrate to four new apps this way, you would have eliminated the presence of four other apps on your device. You will then only be using four instead of eight, which will do wonders for your storage and make organizing those saved files much more convenient.

Naming Conventions

Suppose you have a lot of personal files and photos on your devices. In that case, renaming them will take quite a bit of time, but the benefits you will derive from them are immense. It would help if you got comfortable, put some of your favourite music on a playlist in the background, and use the hourglass method demonstrated in Chapter 4 to reorganize and rename your files in manageable chunks. The benefits of this renaming system will be illustrated as we progress so that the results you can expect to enjoy are precise.

Naming Variants

Final.mp3... Final2.mp3... Final2_Finale.mp3... Final2_Finale_Encore.mp3... Final2_Finale_Encore_Last.mp3... Final2_Finale_Encore_Last_Armageddon.mp3... We have all been there: Having to rename the latest version of a file that we think will be the final version only to end up with a dozen files with the word "Final" in the title that aren't the final version—not even close to being the "final." The first problem with this naming convention is that you never know which version is the final version until the project is done.

Even when the project is supposedly finished, you might revisit it a few weeks later only to make further changes that ensure that the previously saved version is not, in fact, the final version. When sorting these various versions, knowing the chronological sequence of the multiple versions sometimes becomes slightly challenging. You might have decided to go back and make changes to version two, which is far from the latest version of the overall project.

A better way to go about this is simply to use incremental numbers at the very beginning of the file name and to do so using leading zeros. For example, instead of naming a file "Harmony.mp3", call it "001Harmony.mp3." The next version would be named "002Harmony.mp3," and so on.

The advantage of using the leading zeroes at the beginning of the file name is that they will maintain their chronological sequence when the versions are sorted alphabetically. Had you named the first file "1Harmony.mp3" and you ended up making 100 versions of the file, when you tried sorting them alphabetically, "10Harmony.mp3," which is the tenth version of the file, would appear before "2Harmony.mp3" which is the second version of the file.

With the leading zeros naming convention, "002Harmony.mp3" would appear before "010Harmony.mp3" as intended. So, always defaulting to this naming convention is the most efficient way to document and organize different versions of the same original file. To find the final version, you only need to look for the highest leading number from the various versions, which can quickly be found by sorting the files alphabetically.

Rename Memory Lane

Of all the files that most people simply cannot afford to lose, photographs are one of the most important. Once deleted or lost without a backup, there is no way of reversing time to return to that moment with all those people gathered in the same place to recapture that specific moment.

There are also personalized images that we noticed were

extremely prolific when we received feedback from our volunteers regarding their digital decluttering, and these were screenshots. Screenshots seemed to take up more storage space than any other personalized file, and most of the time, these screenshots were rarely revisited.

Go through your screenshots folder and delete as many as possible after first sorting them in the order of the oldest screenshots. You'll find that something that may have seemed important now three years ago has no bearing on your life whatsoever, and these are the files that you can quickly delete to clear up space without reservations.

As for the personal photos saved on your device, the converse is true; the older they are, the more valuable they become. Renaming these files appropriately and backing them up to cloud storage becomes the best way to ensure that you can easily find specific photos when you need them and provides a convenient way of strolling down memory lane.

One such example of an efficient naming technique is to name each photo based on the date the picture was taken, the location, and who is in the photograph. With a quick keyword search, you can find all the images taken on a certain date, at a particular event, or at a particular place without allocating folders and subfolders to sort them.

You can simply have a designated "photos" folder and find the relevant picture using the search function. An example of a file name that uses this naming convention would be "2022_09_13 Berlin Airport Tom Dick Harry 001.jpg." The trailing number at the end follows the same naming convention as the variants naming convention demonstrated in the previous section: It allows you to have multiple images of the same people at the exact location taken on the same date without overwriting other images that carry those same properties.

Remember to back up your photos to cloud storage, as you are usually the only person with those pictures if they were taken on your device. You don't want them to be lost forever should anything happen to that device.

Renaming personal files can be a long process, but one that can be the most rewarding, so you are urged here again to use the hourglass method to break down this take into shorter 15-minute bouts of organizing at a time to make sure and steady progress.

Subscription Subtraction

Sale-Mail
"Congratulations Margret! You are one of the lucky loyal customers eligible for a 50% discount if you spend a minimum of $999 in our online store within the next 5 minutes!" No! This might sound like a fantastic deal; however, it preys on a particular weakness of ADHDers that will be discussed in detail in the following chapter.

Unsubscribing from as many of these spam emails is the best way to declutter your inbox and make it more functional, particularly sales emails with "amazing deals" that require you to make impulsive purchases within a limited time or else you will "miss out" on the offer. Appropriate financial management is far more important than acting on every "deal" in your inbox. Unsubscribe from as many sales-mail and spam emails as possible to make getting to the emails that matter easier.

Browser Extension Extinction

A clogged-up browser is one of the primary culprits that causes your device to start running incredibly slowly and overheat. You can quickly remedy this by clearing your temporary internet files and cache. To make an even more significant impact on your device efficiency, open your browser and navigate to the browser extensions page.

All those active extensions on that page are not only taking up storage space, but they are also eating up your device's processing power. Many of them continue running in the background, even when you may not actively be using that browser extension.

Unless a browser extension is critical and used frequently in your workflow, it is best to delete as many extensions as possible. Even though it is marked as inactive, keeping an extension still takes up space on your device and causes your browser to slow down. Decluttering your extensions will help your device run faster and enable you to complete tasks more quickly without always waiting for apps and programs to load. Do this browser extension decluttering across all the browsers you have on a device if you have more than one browser per device.

Mediocre Media

A subject of online decluttering that gets overlooked, despite being one of the most universal ways to simultaneously remove clutter across all your devices by auditing your online experience, is decluttering the channels and pages you are subscribed to on your social media.

It is every content creator's job to increase engagement with their audience as much as possible, and this can lead to some creators continuously pumping out content that you might not even find beneficial to capitalize on the ad revenue they're awarded each time you view their post.

Of course, there are some channels you may be genuinely interested in following. Still, suppose that the channel posts several posts daily, cluttering your feed. In that case, finding an alternative channel that covers the same topic, but has less frequent but better-curated posts might be best.

Going through your list of liked and followed pages can give you a good idea of which pages are still relevant for you and which pages you might have followed when you were going through a phase. Perhaps you were once getting into a hobby and decided to pursue a dozen pages related to that hobby in a single day. If that hobby no longer interests you, you could substantially clear up your feed to receive more relevant posts by unfollowing and unsubscribing to most, if not all, of those pages.

The critical thing to look out for in assessing which pages to unsubscribe from is their posting frequency and the relevance of those posts to the original reason you subscribed to that channel in the first place.

Pages you still have an interest in that haven't posted in a while due to them taking a hiatus for whatever reason shouldn't be as high a priority for subscription as those making frequent and relevant posts.

The idea here is to audit your overall feed to ensure that you are getting what you want out of these channels as opposed to merely being used as another number to boost their viewership even after they pivot their content to something wholly different and unconstructive to you.

Digital Decluttering: Focus Zone 5

The Goal of This Focus Zone
- Implement the digital decluttering techniques demonstrated in this chapter.

Focus Zone 5 Procedure

1. Set a timer for 15 minutes.

2. Beginning with the app decluttering technique featured in this chapter, set aside 15 minutes daily to implement each of the subtitles outlined.

3. It is advised to start with your cell phone and declutter that device first before moving on to others. This is because you usually carry your mobile phone and have ample opportunities throughout the day to get even more decluttering than the 15 minutes allocated will allow.

Key Chapter Takeaways

- Digitizing essential documents can help in reducing physical clutter.

- Decluttering unused apps on devices will free up space and help the device to run faster.
- Grouping apps on devices can help reduce the number of apps required to complete tasks.
- Organized naming conventions make it easier to find personal files and photographs.
- Using a naming convention with leading zeros for variants makes tracking the latest version saved easier.
- Unsubscribing from "sale-mail" can help reduce impulsivity in spending habits.

Personal finance is one of the taboo topics to discuss in any public forum. It is a stumbling block for many ADHDers, and no book on organizing can be complete without delving into this topic. ADHDers have a unique experience when it comes to finance, and the following chapter will detail these related possible pitfalls and constructive tools and financial strategies you can use.

CHAPTER 6: MONEY MANAGEMENT STRATEGIES

Strength does not come from winning. Your struggles develop your strengths. That is strength when you go through hardships and decide not to surrender. –Arnold Schwarzenegger

Of the 8.7 million adults in the US living with ADHD, the combined socioeconomic cost is around 122.8 billion US dollars, according to a research study funded by the Otsuka Pharmaceutical Development & Commercialization, Inc. That's approximately $14,092 per adult (Schein, 2022).

This is quite a considerable burden for any adult and is even more so when it is placed on the shoulders of those whose symptoms already put them in a habitual state of financial disadvantage by catalyzing economically self-destructive tendencies. This burden initially all seems too theoretical to relate to for neurotypicals, so let us delve deeper to try and understand the impact of ADHD-related symptoms on financial responsibility.

Every Day Is Black Friday!

The best way to describe what ADHD impulsive spending feels like to a neurotypical person is that it is Black Friday every day! You could even stretch that analogy further by saying that Black Friday is the financial equivalent of everyone having ADHD for a day. Of course, there are a lot of nuances to the ADHD experience that neurotypicals don't exhibit.

For one, neurotypicals plan and save up money to spend on Black Friday strategically. But the sentiment is somewhat like that of an ADHDer under the influence of impulsivity; so long as there is a positive bank balance and cash in the wallet or purse, it looks like there are excellent deals everywhere! Everything looks like a bargain, and this is one of the observations that a 2015 Lancet study of 1.92 million people, 32,061 of whom had ADHD, found.

A difficulty in assessing the consequences versus the rewards of specific courses of action contributes to risky and impulsive behaviours, such as impulsive spending. Researchers found that this was one of the factors that resulted in higher mortality rates in adults with ADHD compared to their non-ADHD counterparts (Weiner, 2022).

This chapter will focus on the financial challenges facing people with ADHD through insights graciously shared by our volunteers. It will equip you with various tools and strategies to help you manage your money better without allowing impulsivity to scam you out of your hard-earned funds!

REAL-LIFE STORY # 7

"There was a month I will never forget! I recently got into crypto and was lucky to enter at the right time. A few months later, the markets were up three times, four times, and seven times what I had put in a few months before. So, naturally, I decided to reward myself for being patient and resisting the temptation to withdraw too early. So, I needed to get a new phone, and I found a great deal on a Bluetooth speaker on my way there. And my sister mentioned that she wanted to get some clothes, and I felt generous, so we made it an outing. I wasn't even bothering to check my account balance. I would keep topping it up from crypto and buy whatever I needed. When I checked my statement at the end of the month, I had spent over four months' worth of salary in a single week! I honestly can't even say where the money went. Thanks to my free internet money, I was eating out all the time and talking myself into buying whatever caught my impulsive eye. I eventually found a bit of an extreme solution that works for me, but I think the shock of my inability to take money as seriously as most adults does justify the severity of the financial blockades and hurdles, I have made on purpose." – Aid E.H.D. #3

The most triggering number in the world of adult ADHD is potentially a credit score. The symptom of impulsivity sometimes manifests itself as spending habits that most people would consider nihilistic and reckless. My conversation with the volunteers who offered to share their stories anonymously made me realize how far-reaching the effects of ADHD are in terms of disrupting areas that you would have never thought it could influence.

One of our volunteers explained that he noticed that he would always spend until the money in his account ran out. You would find him at the dollar store if only a dollar were left. Somehow, he interprets a positive account balance as an incomplete task and stops spending once there's nothing left. He explained that the solution he found was to ensure that his bank account remains perpetually empty.

He stores his funds using cryptocurrency and only withdraws when he has made plans and a prior decision to purchase something. It takes him about an hour to do all the administrative work to have the money he needs to make his planned purchases.

It is an extreme measure, to say the least, but granted what I have learned about ADHD and impulsivity, it does make sense. "Speed Breakers," as he calls them, provide him with all the extra hassle and admin required to process the withdrawal, ensuring that it is too much of an inconvenience to spend money impulsively. An adult with ADHD is three times more likely to struggle with debt than their neurotypical counterparts (Jones, 2022).

The percentage of the population who have debt burdens is 11%, which means that if you have ADHD, there is a one in three chance that you will struggle with financial debt in your life. Some with ADHD also have a 49% chance of forming that part of the subgroup who often miss their bills and monthly payments (Beauchaine, 2020).

Impulsive online spending adds yet another spanner to the works. Our volunteer confessed to having to cancel two bank cards because over a dozen monthly subscription charges for apps and Google services used to obliterate his account on the first of the month, and he couldn't trace which specific services he was being charged for.

Engaging with our volunteers gave me a real sense of the pervasiveness of ADHD. The cleaning, decluttering, tidying, and organizing skills did go a long way. Still, to make this book as comprehensive as possible, we must discuss ADHD and finance.

I thought it might be helpful to readers who have ADHD to include a chapter that offers tailored advice for managing this tricky and sensitive subject. This could help in offsetting all the ADHD-related setbacks. So many ADHDers must invent techniques to jostle their way around the world of personal finance, and they shouldn't have to struggle all alone.

Our volunteers suggested covering specific, tangible, and actionable advice would be the most helpful approach. Advising not to be impulsive in your spending is not something you can simply decide to do now. That decision grants your immunity from the real world when spontaneity comes beckoning.

Financial Management Tips and Tools

To provide actionable advice, the following is a list of tools of particular interest to people with ADHD. Some will help you develop good financial habits and become financially organized using the tools. Others are economically helpful in the sense of self-improvement, as they will act as a way for you to reflect on your most recent blunders and renew a monthly vow not to fall for the same perils again.

- **Budgeting app:** Find a monthly budgeting app that can help you track and forecast your monthly spending. If there are any impulsive purchases, the app will help you identify them and recognize potential patterns so that you can avoid them in the future. Some suggestions for such an app are
    - **Hyper Jar:** This app lets you separate your funds into separate jars to keep track of expenses. It also works with Apple Pay; you can schedule payments directly into a specific pot.
    - **Pocket Guard:** This app allows you to set your expense limits and categorize your transactions to understand your monthly cash flow.
    - **EmmaApp:** This app includes a budget and a saving tracking feature. It also allows you to link your accounts for real-time updates.
- **Create a money "to-don't list":** The same recurring issues often wrecked the budget at the beginning of the month. If you'd like to track your progress and make this an exciting project, add the date on each written "to-don't list" and reflect on your progress through this financial journal. By creating a "to-don't list," you can

learn from the mistakes of the previous month and make improvements to the following one. Some examples of things you might include in a "to-don't list" are

  - **Don't** go out partying with a bank card and offer to buy everyone drinks. Instead, take cash.
  - **Don't** ask an Uber driver to wait for you. Waiting charges are expensive!
  - **Don't** sign up for the seven-day "free trial" if they require your banking information. You'll forget to cancel, so that it won't be free.

- **Don't** use your savings to "treat yourself because you deserve it." That's for emergencies only!

- **Automate monthly payments:** The easiest way to remember all your obligations about monthly payments is not to have to remember any of them. Set up debit orders on your bank accounts to automatically pay for things like rent, utility, internet, and cell phone bills. This relieves pressure from remembering which bills have been paid each month and helps automate your budgeting. If possible, it is also a good idea to set up an automatic purchase of grocery store gift cards, especially for students. Two of our volunteers, who are college students, shared their routine struggle of running out of funds for groceries in the middle of the month due to having partied a bit too hard when their allowances came through.

- **Open a savings account:** This isn't the most alluring piece of advice for ADHDers but having a savings account and automating sending some funds to that account each month is one of the best ways to beat the statistics regarding

ADHDers in severe debt. Having no savings is only one step away from falling into debt. Even if you aren't amassing a small fortune, depleting your savings can become a healthy guardrail that alerts you when your spending has gotten out of control. The associated stress of the battle to replenish your savings is far better than that of trying to pay off accumulated debt. Setting your allocated savings amount as a percentage of your income rather than a fixed amount is a great way to ensure that your given savings increase in proportion to your income, and this also encourages you to live below your means even as those means continue to grow.

- **Cash is critical:** Withdraw a fixed amount for your weekly spending instead of carrying a credit card. It is straightforward to lose track of impulsive spreading until it is too late with a card. When you look at your weekly statement, the damage has already been done, and your impulsivity may have gotten the better of you. Opening your purse or wallet to have a direct visual cue of how much cash you started with and the rate at which that stack of notes decreases provides you with a constant feedback system. You will find yourself wisely having second thoughts before making an impulsive purchase when you open your wallet and do some quick math on how far along in the week you are and how much cash you have remaining.

Adhd Tax

ADHDers across the board can relate to the concept of the "ADHD tax." Whether it is the extra funds that you need to pay for therapy appointments, which don't come cheap, the monthly money that needs to be set aside for paying for medication, or even the tax on time and energy that comes from taking a few extra years to graduate from college because of either having to repeat courses because of failing due to late assignments, or simply changing the course being studied due to a dwindling interest in the current course, ADHDers end up paying more in terms of time, energy, emotional toll, and financial burdens that neurotypical people aren't faced with.

This results in having less disposable income and a temptation to escape from reality through impulsive spending or hyper focusing on a new hobby. That new hobby can lead to the ADHDer spending significant money purchasing all the equipment, software, and start-up tools required to get going, only to lose interest and have that investment accumulate dust in a doom pile somewhere. Procrastination can lead to putting off medical or dental concerns until they reach crisis point, resulting in paying thousands in bills.

In contrast, those concerns could have been addressed with far less money had they been addressed in time. Forgetting to pay bills on time habitually will negatively impact an ADHDer's credit score, leading to them paying higher interest rates when they apply for loans.

These prospects may seem bleak, but it is helpful to keep in mind the considerable odds working against you as someone with ADHD. These can act as a source of motivation in your drive to go the extra mile to ensure that you take additional financial precautions even though those around you might not be doing the same. Remember, you are playing the same economic game. Still, the rules are set to work in your favour, so it will take a concerted effort to form healthy habits to counteract those rules.

Hormonal Changes

This may seem like a seemingly random point to address this issue. Still, there are many cases of middle-aged women who begin to feel suddenly overwhelmed by life and are losing control in multiple areas, including finances. This has them consulting a physician, fearing that these sudden terrifying experiences could be the signs of early-onset Alzheimer's disease. This is often when high-functioning women who have been misdiagnosed and treated for stress and anxiety their whole lives finally come to the correct diagnosis of their ADHD.

Finances can significantly impact well-being and overall lifestyle in that they trigger a deep dive into diagnosing the root cause of suddenly feeling like you're "losing it" regarding your ability to manage. The compounding effects of decreased estrogen levels in women in midlife and lowered dopamine levels because of untreated and undiagnosed ADHD create the perfect storm. This perfect storm manifests through the decimated finances of middle-aged women as they compare how they fared earlier on in life with the turn things seem to be taking. This is accompanied by sudden inadequacy and feeling misunderstood after a lifetime of fighting a valiant battle against an invisible, anonymous enemy.

Cognitive-related symptoms in premenopausal women are mainly more pronounced in undiagnosed women with ADHD. If it did take a financial calamity to reach your diagnosis finally, that is nothing to be ashamed of. On the contrary, you can now have peace of mind knowing that the issue is finally being remedied. You can also find solace in the fact that this issue is being addressed in the finance section of this book and take this as reassurance that it is a common occurrence in undiagnosed women who share your neurological condition.

ADHD Disability Benefits

While talking about the often-taboo topics surrounding finance and ADHD, it would be irresponsible not to mention that there is financial aid available for those who are genuinely struggling with employment and ADHD or the added bills that come with having children who have ADHD. ADHD is a hereditary disease, which means that the likelihood of your children having ADHD is high if you, as the biological parent, have ADHD. This additional financial strain can be relieved by applying for benefits to cover you or your child.

Suppose you have severe ADHD and are unable to work for reasons related to your condition. In that case, you may be entitled to benefits from your Social Security Disability Insurance. Suppose you have previously worked for a long enough time to have paid Social Security taxes and cannot do substantial gainful activity (SGA).

In that case, you can apply for Social Security benefits for your condition. Even if you are gainfully employed but have children with ADHD that require additional expenses such as medication and therapy appointments, you could be entitled to Social Security benefits. You are advised to consult with your attorney to determine the local laws and procedures to access these supplementary resources (*ADHD & disability benefits*, n.d.)

REAL-LIFE STORY # 8

"Tech has been the biggest financial headache for me. It's not so much the impulsive spending that gets me every time, but rather the impulsive signing up to platforms and subscriptions that offer a 'free two-week trial' and then ask for your credit card details. Of course, the plan is always to sign up and cancel before the free trial ends. Still, some of these sites are things I sign up for impulsively because there's a specific audiobook that I will get to listen to for free, or there's a specific article I want to read quickly, and then I'll sign out. The problem is that when I forget, and those debit orders start wrecking my bank account, I can't remember what site or specific service is charging me because it gets charged under the name of a different parent company, or sometimes it will just read 'Google Services' being charged five times at five different prices, and I then must block my card and create a new one. I once even had to shut down my bank account because of too many monthly charges going off from kind of anonymous sources, but I have since learned of the beauty of online virtual cards that you can set up specifically for signing up purposes and then simply cancel the card without having to shut down your entire bank account if unwanted charges start coming in out of nowhere."
–Aid E.H.D. #4

An interesting fact that most people aren't aware of is

that the English word "mirror" has the exact Latin origin of the Spanish word "mirror," which means "to look." This makes perfect sense as the entire purpose of a mirror, in most cases, is to look at yourself: to see how others see you or to look at yourself more objectively from the outside.

The reasons for this are obvious: If you have something stuck in your hair, or you have something on your chin that you need to wipe off, or even if it is no other reason than that you're about to go out and would like to make sure you're looking your best, mirrors are helpful.

If there were a set of identical twins and one refused to use mirrors while the other used them often, you would see the difference. The twins not using the mirror would assume that they still look as good as their twin sibling, utterly oblivious to how unkempt they had allowed themselves to become due to a lack of visual feedback that the mirror provides.

The twin who *is* using mirrors would be encouraged to do so even more because they can see the difference between how they would look if they were unkempt by looking at their sibling and how they appear now that they comb their hair, wash their face, and make themselves look presentable before stepping out into the world.

Whether we like it or not, the world will not treat the two the same. Although they may feel the same way inside, the world will initially judge based on the bottom line, the results, or, in this case, the appearance.

Similarly, not regularly checking in to look at your finances is like being an unkempt twin who has allowed their inability to take an objective look at themselves in the mirror to become a genuine disadvantage in terms of their ability to function in the world. It only adds hurdles that needn't be there.

Getting into the habit of *regularly and routinely* checking your financial statements will allow you to notice when you have "something stuck in your hair" that month. Not looking in that mirror doesn't change the fact that you have a twig stuck in your hair; in fact, it only makes matters worse as you will be walking around looking like that until someone musters up the courage to tell you that there is something stuck in your hair.

Unfortunately, personal finance is a somewhat taboo topic, which means things will often have to go very wrong before someone else is brave enough to confront you to get your finances in order.

You can easily spare yourself such an uncomfortable interaction by taking the initiative to engage yourself. As is always the case with organizing, that purpose is not to punish yourself but to help yourself to function more efficiently. There will be weeks when you look at that statement and don't like what you see. Still, the advantage here lies in that the sooner you've spotted an issue, the sooner you can take measures to remedy that issue.

As was the case with our volunteer's story above, some financial issues are so nuanced that the best advice to offer is centered around the principle that will guide you in engineering your tailored solution. In this case, the principle is to check in on your account statements weekly, see where some excess spending is creeping in, and try to find ways to mitigate those economic leakages in the future.

Money Management: Focus Zone 6

The Goal of This Focus Zone
- Create your "to-don't list."

Focus Zone 6 Procedure

1. Set a timer for 15 minutes.

2. Print out a copy of your bank statements from the past six months.

3. Go through the list of all the transactions and highlight any transactions that you believe were linked to impulsive spending.

4. Using these highlighted transactions as inspiration, get a notepad and write today's date and the title "to-don't list."

5. Write down your first monthly "to-don't list" based on the instructions issued earlier in this chapter.

6. Repeat this exercise each month and add a note as to your progress and successes in avoiding the pitfalls of the previous month.

Key Chapter Takeaways

- Creating and implementing a monthly budget using an app to track spending is crucial for having healthy finances.

- Creating a "to-don't list" helps track episodes of impulsive spending from month to month.

- Withdrawing cash each week is better than using a card, where spending is harder to track and see.

- There are Social Security benefits available for parents with children who have ADHD, and this can be used to supplement the compounded costs of parent and child medical bills (medication and therapy appointments).

- Automating monthly payments can help you to pay bills on time and, thus, improve your credit score.

Now that we have paid sufficient attention to finance, we can finally address the elephant in the room regarding ADHD: the issue of distraction and, more specifically, digital distractions. How can they best be managed, and what measures can be put into place so as not to fall victim to them? That is precisely what will be covered in the following chapter.

CHAPTER 7: DIGITAL DISTRACTIONS

Thinking is good for your mind, but too much thinking leads to distraction. –Elie Habib

REAL-LIFE STORY # 9

"It was the university holidays, so I travelled back home to visit my family. One evening, while eating supper at the dinner table, my father asked my brother if he could cut the lawn the following day. We would host a small family get-together on the weekend, and the place had to look presentable. My brother then pointed out that he hadn't done it already because the lawnmower had some sort of engine issue and needed to be taken in for service. Since I was the only one with a driver's license who would be home the next day, I offered to get it repaired during the day so my brother could sort out the lawn later. I didn't think to set a reminder on my phone for this. The following day, just past noon, my brother came to remind me about the needed repairs. I had completely forgotten! I grabbed the lawnmower, took it to the car, and opened the rear door to put it in, and that's when I realized that I needed to get some newspapers to lay down to protect the car's interior. I headed back inside. A few hours later, while scrolling through my social media, I noticed it was getting dark, and my brother still hadn't started mowing the lawn like he had *said.*

Feeling entirely annoyed by having to nag him to do a simple chore, I went to his room to confront him about it. As I entered, he exclaimed, 'Oh, you're back already? I didn't hear you leaving in the car.' I was confused but focused on the matter: 'It's late, and you still haven't started with the lawn. Dad will be fuming!' to which he replied, 'I was waiting for you to come back from fixing the lawnmower.' And then it hit me.

I returned to the garage to find the car's rear door still open, the lawnmower positioned and ready to be loaded in after I had laid down the newspapers. That's the day I learned to always have a visual cue in my field of vision to remind me of important tasks. The second I re-entered the house to get those newspapers, my brain was swarmed by a thousand other things. It's not that an ADHD brain struggles to complete tasks, but instead that it works to fight the urge to start a dozen new ones." –Aid E.H.D. #2

Distraction Minimizing Techniques

In this chapter, we will look closer into methods of minimizing digital distractions as much as possible. The digital world poses a more significant threat of distraction as the content consumed online these days is only limited by your curiosity. From what I have seen through my interactions with our volunteers, ADHDers are *extremely* curious and creative people.

ADHDers often have a roster of very different and unrelated, very particular niche topics, hobbies, and interests that they can discuss with the competence of semi-professionals in those subjects. That's a testament to how far ADHDers follow the rabbit hole when they decide to go into a topic. Our task now is to regulate that hyperfocus by managing digital distractions to ensure that your curiosity doesn't carry you away involuntarily and leave you with the anxiety of having insufficient time to complete your essential tasks.

Boarding Pass

After speaking to all our volunteers to determine which methods they found most effective when shutting out digital distractions to focus on work, one extreme lateral-thinking initiative came up twice: airplane mode. All cell phones and most digital devices have this feature. It is beneficial when it comes to cell phones. Activating airplane mode on your phone allows you to keep your cell phone on while completely blocking all incoming calls and messages as though your phone is off. We learned that activating the airplane mode on a cell phone during a call will result in a "call failed" notification on the other end instead of a "call ended" notification. This feature takes your phone off the grid for as long as it is active. It lets you focus on the task while eliminating the possibility of receiving notifications from incoming messages and calls.

After deactivating airplane mode, all the messages and missed call notifications that came in while it was active will all come through, and you can then attend to them accordingly. This has proven extremely useful for the volunteers who used this method, and the others who started using it after discovering it through this project also found it beneficial.

It creates a routine before committing to focusing on work. It tricks your brain into thinking that you are going away on a trip for the next few hours. You will be unavailable to respond to incoming communication, so communication must simply wait. Suppose the world can continue spinning without imploding when you activate airplane mode to board a flight. In that case, it can continue when you voluntarily start the feature to focus on a task.

App Tracking

Most tablets and mobile phones also have a feature that allows you to track how much time is spent daily on the various apps on your device. This data is broken down into percentages and hours. Some tablets and cell phones allow you to use this tracking feature to limit your time on any given app per day. You can think of it as a chronological budget.

Once you hit the limit of this daily time budget for a specific app for the day, that app will automatically close. You can only open it again after midnight when the daily time budget refreshes.

Gone are the days when you find yourself aimlessly scrolling through TikTok only to get anxiously awakened by the reality that several unproductive hours have gone by without you attending to more urgent matters. Now, you can turn that source of distraction into your greatest ally. Set daily time limits on apps like TikTok, Instagram, Netflix, and Facebook, and make it a reasonable allotment of time-based on looking through how much time you've spent on these apps on average throughout the week.

The hidden danger behind setting up unrealistic expectations with these limits is that if you usually spend an average of three hours per day on Netflix and suddenly try to cut that down to only one hour daily, you are more likely to protest yourself.

You will just reset the limit and increase it when it is reached because a part of you will think it unreasonable to set such an unrealistic expectation in the first place. If the limit placed is fair and reasonable, then when the time restriction shuts the app down, you are much more likely to abide by that restriction. You will be aware that you are being unreasonable in that instance for wanting to continue indulging in that app beyond the permitted time.

The idea here is to catch yourself when you're about to fall victim to the time blindness that we discussed in Chapter 4 of this book. You want to make yourself immediately aware of the moments where you start to veer off course and run the risk of getting sidetracked beyond redemption, not punish yourself for daring to take healthy breaks throughout the day.

Sorry to Burst Your Bubbles

Bursting bubbles can give us a quick dopamine rush throughout the day. Still, they can also be a gateway to other distractions. Whenever these digital bubbles appear as pop-up notifications, updating us with how many messages await our attention within various apps, we immediately open those apps and read through those notifications to "burst" those bubbles.

People may be liking your post or even showering you with compliments and words of congratulation. It becomes a vicious cycle because the more we attend to these notifications and respond to these interactions, the more people will interact with our comments on their comments. This avalanche of interaction becomes a full-time distraction from other more pressing issues that require our focus.

These pop-up notifications also feed a lot into impulsivity. You no longer get to decide when to open a particular app. Still, you are cordially invited to do so every half an hour by a new pop-up bubble that appears begging to burst as soon as possible. Your brain is tricked into a false sense of urgency where the urgency doesn't indeed exist! These notifications can surely wait.

To turn these tables around and go from being used by social media to being a social media user, you must take complete control of when you open any given app. This means setting a clear boundary by not allowing apps to summon you without restraint the moment it suits a platform to command your attention. It may seem drastic initially but turning off your app notifications is the best way to ensure you always remain in control. This doesn't mean that you're deleting your account or that you will miss any important notifications.

It simply means that you refuse to get distracted by the constant influx of pop-up bubbles begging to be burst and distracting you from whatever task you have decided to focus on at any given time. You will still attend to those notifications, as you have before. Still, you will do so this time when you choose to open that app, not when it summons you.

This can quickly be done by navigating to your phone settings and turning off notifications for each app. Of course, this should not be applied to your work apps, as these notification pop-ups would generally fall under the urgent and important quadrant. Still, all other app's pop-up notifications can be turned off. Those notifications can wait until you decide you have the time to open the apps to attend to them.

Grappling With Algorithms

Every social media site makes use of algorithms. These algorithms are computer codes designed to analyze what content you have engaged with and watched to predict what other similar content you're most likely to find interesting. Therefore, sometimes landing on your homepage on a site like YouTube can become a lot more distracting. The algorithm has had time to analyze your previous activity to welcome you with the content you predict will find most irresistible when you return to your home page. The best way to maneuver around this pitfall is to avoid using the platform's default home page altogether. Instead, bookmark the page that shows updates from your subscribed channels and always navigate to that page. This ensures that you start seeing what you came there for instead of being immediately tempted into a rabbit hole by a witty algorithm programmed to manipulate your next move.

Digital Distractions: Focus Zone 7

The Goal of This Focus Zone
- Implement restrictions on permitted app time usage.
- Remove all pop-up notifications for apps unrelated to work.

Focus Zone 7 Procedure

1. Set a timer for 15 minutes.

2. Navigate to the app usage setting on your most used devices.

3. Analyze your average daily spending habits on the various apps and set up time restrictions for each app to limit the average hours that the app is used per day (this will, in effect, lower your average usage of the apps).

4. For each app that currently sends you pop-up

notifications, navigate to its settings and turn off all notifications.

Key Chapter Takeaways

- Switching your phone to "airplane mode" is a helpful way to shut out all digital distractions, allowing you to focus.

- Setting daily time limits for how long you are permitted to use recreational apps can help you to avoid getting sucked into distracting "rabbit holes" by accident.

- Disabling push notifications for recreational apps will allow you to focus and control when you open those apps.

- Avoid navigating to home pages of social media sites where algorithms curate distracting content: Bookmark your subscribed challenge feed instead and navigate there directly.

CONCLUSION

Everything will be okay in the end. If it's not okay, it's not the end. –John Lennon

It really and indeed has been an insightful journey for me. Little did I know when responding to those emails a few months ago that my journey would lead me here. Not only did I connect with the volunteers, but I extended that journey to connect with you, the reader, the unseen volunteer who joined us in our journey and had your life blitzcluttered and organized into shape as you followed along with the Focus Zone exercises. You, too, have your own stories and anecdotes, which I'm sure would make for a fantastic read in another book!

I would love to thank all our volunteers who shared their personal stories and allowed me into their world, or your world, as ADHDers. I trust this book will help many others see that change is possible. Though the odds may be stacked against you in some respects, the resilience, positivity, curiosity, and creativity that I witnessed when working with ADHDers convinced me that there truly is nothing that an ADHDer cannot achieve if they set that fascinating mind to it.

The journey is not complete but ongoing. To succeed with

the methods outlined in this book, you may need to read and reread it and continue implementing the techniques and principles shared here daily. I would love to hear if any of these techniques inspired you to create effective variations of these exercises. Who knows? Your emails might just plant the seeds of part two in this literary adventure!

THANK YOU

I would like to really thank you for reading my book till the end, and most importantly, apply as much as you can from what you learned here. As nothing would make me happier than knowing that someone's life is getting better because of something I shared!

I consider myself leveraged because you chose my book over all the other books to discover.

So, THANK YOU for purchasing this book and for making it all the way to here.

Before you leave, I would like to ask for a favour! **Could you please share one or two things you learned or liked about this book in a review? That would really help me continue sharing more knowledge and would show your support to an independent author like myself!**

Your opinion will assist and encourage me to keep writing and publishing useful content to more people, hoping to make more people happier and enjoy their dream lives. Hearing from you would mean so much to me.

>> **Leave a review on Amazon US** <<
>> **Leave a review on Amazon UK** <<

REFERENCES

ADHD & disability benefits. (n.d.). Paul Baker Law Offices. https://pbakerlaw.com/social-security-lawyers/adhd-disability-benefits-for-adults/

Armstrong, T. (1999). ADD/ADHD alternatives in the classroom. Association for Supervision and Curriculum Development.

Beauchaine, T. P., Ben-David, I., & Bos, M. (2020). ADHD, financial distress, and suicide in adulthood: A population study. Science Advances, 6(40), eaba1551. https://doi.org/10.1126/sciadv.aba1551

Bismarck, O. (n.d.). Otto von Bismarck quotes. Goodreads. https://www.goodreads.com/quotes/79541-fools-learn-from-experience-i-prefer-to-learn-from-

Durand, G., Arbone, I.-S., & Wharton, M. (2020). Reduced organizational skills in adults with ADHD are due to deficits in persistence, not in strategies. PeerJ, 8, e9844. https://www.ncbi.nlm.nih.gov/pmc/articles/PMC7485505/

Habib, E. (n.d.). Elie Habib quotes. https://www.quotemaster.org/qf0d23c7d668a816bb825e1f68567e657

Jones, R. (2022, June 25). "Shopping is a nightmare": how ADHD affects people's spending habits. The Guardian. https://www.theguardian.com/money/2022/jun/25/shopping-adhd-spending-habits#:~:text=Those%20with%20ADHD%20are%20almost

Lennon, J. (n.d.). John Lennon quotes. Goodreads. https://www.goodreads.com/quotes/628927-everything-will-be-okay-in-the-end-if-it-s-not

Mayer, K. (n.d.). Katrina Mayer quotes. Guideposts. https://guideposts.org/positive-living/health-and-wellness/life-advice/managing-life-changes/8-motivational-quotes-for-decluttering/

Renard, J. (n.d.). Jules Renard quotes. Goodreads. https://www.goodreads.com/work/quotes/3704049-journal-1887-1910

Richards, C. (n.d.). Charles Richards quotes. Goodreads. https://www.goodreads.com/author/quotes/452105.Charles_Richards#:~:text=Charles%20Richards%20Quotes&text=There%20are%20only%20as%20many,as%20you%20make%20use%20of.&text=10-,Don't%20be%20fooled%20by%20the%20calendar.,value%20out%20of%20a%20week.

Schein, J., Adler, L. A., Childress, A., Gagnon-Sanschagrin, P., Davidson, M., Kinkead, F., Cloutier, M., Guérin, A., & Lefebvre, P. (2022). Economic burden of attention-deficit/hyperactivity disorder among adults in the United States: a societal perspective. Journal of Managed Care & Specialty Pharmacy, 28(2), 168–179. https://doi.org/10.18553/jmcp.2021.21290

Schwarzenegger, A. (n.d.). Arnold Schwarzenegger quotes. Brainyquote. https://www.brainyquote.com/quotes/arnold_schwarzenegger_116694

Tzu, L. (n.d.). Tao Te Ching quotes. Goodreads. https://www.goodreads.com/quotes/1339572-when-the-student-is-ready-the-teache

Weiner, M. (2022, December 4). Time blindness: an ADHD symptom that can harm your finances. Health. https://www.health.com/condition/adhd/time-blindness-impulsive-spending-adhd-symptoms

ABOUT THE AUTHOR

Kai M. Jordan

Kai M. Jordan is an author in the field of self-development, home management and lifestyle coach. Visit http://swenettbooks.com and get access to Kai's Decluttering Bundle for FREE.

In her books, Kai shares over ten years of practical knowledge and the timeless wisdom she learned from an early age about managing homes, mind and life by self-discovery, and self-management. She turns these life lessons into actionable steps to help you develop a healthy relationship with yourself, with others, and ultimately with life itself.

In her honest and inspiring books, Kai talks about what she believes are the obstacles to living the life you desire. She shares best practices to help you declutter your home, mind & life, improve powerful habits, erase negativity, control anxiety, reduce overthinking, and minimize any expectations of others. She guides YOU to think, decide and become the best version of yourself.

Kai studied business administration and project management. When she's not on her mission to make people's life better, she loves to read, meditate, workout, and take long walks in nature.

BOOKS BY THIS AUTHOR

Decluttering Your Home In A Year Or Less! Workbook

Declutter Your Mind In A Year Or Less!

Organize Your Digital Life

Organize Your Home In A Year Or Less!

Thrive With Adult Adhd Workbook For Women

www.ingramcontent.com/pod-product-compliance
Lightning Source LLC
LaVergne TN
LVHW041254080426
835510LV00009B/726